Singing We Go

FIFTY YEARS WITH THE WOODVALE

AMBASSADOR

BELFAST ◆ **GREENVILLE**
NORTHERN IRELAND   SOUTH CAROLINA

FIFTY YEARS WITH THE WOODVALE
Copyright © 1998 Victor Maxwell with The Woodvale

ISBN 1 84030 041 8

Ambassador Publications
a division of
Ambassador Productions Ltd.
Providence House
16 Hillview Avenue,
Belfast, BT5 6JR
Northern Ireland

Emerald House
1 Chick Springs Road, Suite 203
Greenville,
South Carolina 29609, USA

www.emeraldhouse.com

Contents

CHAPTER ONE

Farther Along

--------------------------- ❖ ---------------------------

**BELFAST'S MAGNIFICENT CONCERT HALL, THE
WATERFRONT, APPROPRIATELY NAMED BECAUSE**
of its location on the northern bank of the River Lagan, was
packed to capacity. The audience had come from all over Ulster
and some families had flown in from England and Scotland.
When two thousand people of all ages had settled into their
plush seats the warm glow of the Hall's concealed lighting
dimmed and the stage lights flashed into life. Bright beams
from the spot lights focused on many local Christian artists
and a large backing chorus who had filed onto the stage. They
had all come to make their contribution to a great evening of
praise, a Gospel Homecoming Concert.

The choir burst into song in support of Rev. William
McCrea as he enthusiastically sang one of his rousing gospel
hymns accompanied by a variety of string and percussion
instruments. He was followed by other singers who made their

musical and vocal contributions singing, *Sweet Beulah Land, I Feel like Travelling Home* and *In My Father's House Above.* Soon it became evident that heaven was the theme of all the musical selections as Nell Hire, Paul and Sharon Gardiner, Sharon Mills, Karen Marsden and the Zionaires sang with great warmth and enthusiasm.

The Palmetto Quartet from Greenville, South Carolina, USA, eloquently blended in harmony to sing some of the great Southern gospel songs that express the beauties of *Our Heavenly Home.* The musical accompaniment of the local artists as well as an outstanding presentation on the piano of *When I Survey the Wondrous Cross* by Lari Goss, one of America's most respected musicians who had flown in from Nashville, USA, was superb. Each piece was greeted by rapturous applause by the audience which sometimes joined in singing some of the better known songs.

Midway through the programme Belfast's own Woodvale Quintet, known throughout Ulster and beyond, took their place at the microphones at centre stage. Smartly dressed in matching blazers and trousers with co-ordinated ties, they were enthusiastically greeted by warm applause from the very responsive audience. Although the five singers are well known to any Christian congregation in Ulster, Alec McCarroll, the Quintet's tenor and longest serving member, took time to introduce each of his colleagues.

Denis Kennedy, the second tenor, has been singing with the group for twenty-nine years. His voice is still as mellow as when he first began. Ian Mawhinney, a baritone, is the most recent vocal recruit to the Woodvale and his voice brings great quality to the over all sound. Harry Oliver sat in front of a microphone at the piano from where he sang as the lead baritone. Harry's velvet-like and confident voice with its rich and smooth resonance blended superbly with his soft touch on the piano keyboard. Young Richard Crawford played an electric guitar in accompaniment with the Quintet. George Whitely, the second bass, is older than the other men in the Quintet. His wit, humour and charisma make George a favourite with audiences wherever the Woodvale Quintet sing. He has been with the Woodvale for over thirty-five years and was often the speaker when they were invited to minister the Word of God.

Alec announced their first song, *Where No One Stands Alone*. At a signal which was imperceptible to most, the boys began to sing with amazing blend and harmony:

Once I stood in the night,
With my head bowed down,
In the darkness as black as could be,
And my heart felt alone,
And I cried 'O Lord
Don't hide your face from me.'

Hold my hand all the way,
Every hour, every day,
From here to the great unknown,
Take my hand, let me stand,
Where no one stands alone.

Like a King I may live,
In a palace so tall,
With great riches to claim as my own,
But I don't know a thing,
In the whole wide world,
That's worse than losing your soul.

The lyrics were clear and the message was inspiring. The five voices increased in volume swelling towards a final crescendo. The backing sound and tempo enhanced the build-up. The climax was majestic. Sustained rapturous applause rang throughout the theatre.

The Woodvale remained on their feet as all the artists and the accompanying choir burst into song with an old gospel quartet favourite, *Farther Along We'll Know All About It.*

> Tempted and tried we're oft made to wonder
> Why it should be thus all the day long,
> While there are others living about us
> Never molested, though in the wrong.

> *"Farther along we'll know all about it*
> *Farther along we'll understand why*
> *Cheer up my brother live in the sunshine*
> *We'll understand it all bye and bye."*

This was not the first time for the Woodvale men to sing this famous quartet hymn. They had been singing the same lyrics for almost fifty years.

Farther Along was an appropriate song for the occasion. Alec McCarroll had been with the group for all that time. He had come a long way from the early and humble beginnings of the Woodvale Quintet which commenced unobtrusively when a group of four boys gathered round an old stove in a North Belfast Mission Hall to blend their voices in song. They were trying to emulate the sound of some favourite singing groups they had heard in the years just following the Second World War.

At that time Belfast was greatly blessed with an abundance of male voice choirs as well as some musical groups which engaged in singing the gospel in many churches and mission halls. These groups were largely made up of working class men who gave their free time to do what they loved best, singing about their Lord and Saviour.

Such men were Jock and Walter McCormick who worked for the Belfast Transport Corporation based in Napier Street, off Sandy Row. Andy Poots, Bob McCartney and Vincey Morrison, like the McCormick brothers, were ordinary working men who lived nearby on the Donegall Road. This band of Christian men started to sing in the Donegall Road City Mission in 1931. Soon they became known as the Donegall Road Singers and for the next forty-two years they sang the gospel all over Northern Ireland. During the dark days leading up to the Second World War they brightened many Sunday evening services as they sang some of the great gospel songs of that generation in wonderful harmony.

In those years the world was overshadowed by the Great Depression which brought economic collapse to the world's leading economies. Europe was trying to cope with the growing menace of Hitler who was sweeping to power in Germany, while Mussolini ran the show in Italy, and General Franco suppressed and liquidated the opposition in Spain.

During those bewildering years Belfast city was dominated by several great industries: the Harland and Wolff shipyards, the largest of its kind in the world; the Belfast Rope Works which had also gained world-wide fame and the famous Linen and Spinning Mills on the Crumlin and Falls Roads. These industries were the backbone of employment for tens of thousands of people who lived in the tightly compacted streets of terraced houses adjacent to and often overshadowed by these great centres of industry.

Two of Belfast's more famous thoroughfares were the Shankhill and Crumlin Roads which ascended as parallel routes out of the town centre heading north toward the imposing Black Mountain. The mountain overlooked the city below which is cradled in the picturesque Lagan Valley. Between these two main roads was a labyrinth of short streets of terraced houses and several schools where hundreds of local children gained their education. Four of these children were young boys who became pals during their formative scholastic and adolescent years.

Two of these boys attended two of these schools, Edenderry Intermediate School on Tennent Street and Glenwood Intermediate School on the Shankhill Road. Alec McCarroll was a lean red-haired boy from Walton Street. Harry Yates lived close by in Palmer Street on the opposite side of the Crumlin Road. The height of their ambition was to leave school at fourteen years old and find their fortune in one of the nearby industries. Usually a boy's fourteenth birthday also coincided with what was referred to in the jargon of the day as, "sliding down the banister" that is, graduating from short pants into long trousers. They were like most boys of their time who during the long summer evenings spent their free time playing football on the street or trying a hand at cricket in the nearby Woodvale Park.

In contrast to the youth of our present time, the peak of any illegal activity was dodging the local bobby on the beat so that the boys could enjoy a game of football against a broad gable wall at any street corner. These games were played with great zest and earnestness. Instead of a soccer ball they used a small tennis ball. Sometimes a well intentioned but misdirected kick of the ball incurred the wrath of a neighbour when the ball missed the goal and whistled through a window. At the sound of breaking glass the boys didn't wait around for their ball but instead they sped down an alley to avoid the anger and threats of an irate neighbour. On other occasions they played a more benign game of soccer - the ball was made from a few pair of father's old socks, or even at times a tin can could be heard being kicked by a gang of boys.

Andy Taggart, another of the four friends, pursued other sports with some success. As a boy he joined the Windsor Boxing Club where he proved to have the ability to take him to the top of this very physical sport. As Andy developed his sparring skills he was taken under the wing of Mr. Dan McAllister, a distinguished trainer at the time. Under Mr. McAllister's guidance and coaching Andy went on to win many local titles and eventually became the Irish Bantam Weight Champion.

On one occasion Andy fought the legendary "Spider" (Billy) Kelly, one of Northern Ireland's greats in the boxing arena. Although I am not sure who won the fight, it is sufficient to say that afterwards Andy Taggart became a competent cross-country runner. Again he distinguished himself as a runner and won several medals and championships in athletics.

John Adams attended Edenderry Intermediate School. He completed the foursome of companions who as boys chummed with each other and later in life would make a great impact on evangelical life in Northern Ireland.

John was always a very serious minded fellow. He lived not far from Andy's home and after he left school at fourteen years old he went to work in the reeling room at Ewart's Spinning Mill on the Crumlin Road. At the Mill he met up with Alec McCarroll's mother and consequently kept in touch with Alec.

Scattered throughout the Shankhill and Crumlin Road area were many churches of various denominations with fine buildings and pointed steeples. On Sunday mornings these churches were packed by well dressed worshippers, many of whom unashamedly carried their Bibles to and from their places of worship. Sunday was strictly regarded as a day of rest. All shops and the local Woodvale Park's sports area were firmly closed. Most children crowded into Sunday School in a local church or in one of many mission halls. Nearly all these halls were erected to compliment the evangelistic work of the churches in the community and therefore they convened their meetings on Sunday evenings as well as on other week nights.

Over and above their evangelistic work, the local mission halls played an important role in the social life of the district. Here neighbours met and got acquainted with each other. Local news and chatter were often exchanged and lasting friendships were formed. Sometimes the halls were warmer and more comfortable than the crowded and drafty two bedroom houses where the locals lived.

The mission halls were known for their bright singing and evangelistic preaching, often by local laymen who had no formal theological training. Soloists and singing groups were given opportunity to employ their musical talents to convey the great gospel themes. Belfast had several famous Christian male voice choirs who also frequented these halls on a regular basis and sang with great blend and harmony their joyful chorus of gospel songs.

With such enthusiastic and evangelistic activity it is not surprising that some of the halls were better frequented than the churches. The mission hall was often the place where people were converted to Christ, introduced to the Christian life and integrated into Christian work. One of these mission halls was to play a big part in the life and witness of the four young lads who had been fellow pupils at the Edenderry and Everton Schools.

One night when Alec McCarroll was only a boy he was dumbfounded to hear the roar of German aircraft flying over Belfast. He never forgot when the dark skies over Belfast were lit up with the explosion of a German incendiary bomb which made a direct hit on the Crumlin Road Presbyterian Church on the opposite side of the road from his home. To young Alec it seemed the whole street was ablaze. He watched with wide eyes as uniformed firemen firmly holding their hose pipes doused thousands of gallons of water in a vain attempt to extinguish the leaping flames. It seemed like an inferno, a veritable lake of fire.

The houses in the adjoining Ewart's Row were also ablaze and some neighbours had been incinerated in the flame. The Ewart's Row houses formed a two story barrier which sheltered Walton Street from the main force of the blast. In the providence of God, the McCarroll family and the other residents of Walton Street were spared from a what would have been a sure and grim end. It was a frightening experience that was so etched on Alec's young mind that every time he walked down Walton Street he seemed to re-live that dreadful night. He could almost feel his mop of ginger hair stand on end at the thought of the horrific flames.

Shortly after this dreadful incident the McCarroll family moved from Walton Street to Montreal Street on the other side of the Crumlin Road. While at Walton Street Alec attended Beechpark City Mission Sunday School but due to this move he was located nearer to the Woodvale Mission on Disraeli Street. Peggy McClean was his teacher at this new Sunday School. A Sunday School teacher's work is a long term investment. Neither Alec nor Peggy was aware that the precious truths of the gospel which she taught in those impressionable years would shape Alec's life and subsequently touch thousands of people.   Farther along they would learn all about it.

> Faithful till death, said our loving Master,
> A few more days to labour and wait;
> Toils of the road will then seem as nothing,
> As we sweep through the beautiful gate.

"Farther along we'll know all about it
Farther along we'll understand why
Cheer up my brother live in the sunshine
We'll understand it all bye and bye."

When we see Jesus coming in glory,
When He comes from His Home in the sky,
Then we shall meet Him in that bright mansion
We'll understand it all bye and bye.

CHAPTER TWO

Who Can Cheer The Heart?

❖

**WHILE AT SCHOOL IT BECAME EVIDENT THAT
ALEC HAD A SWEET TENOR VOICE. SOON HE WAS**
selected to sing solo parts in many school productions. At the
same school and in the same class Isobel Morrow was also a
pupil. She had a very rich voice which in later years would
make her one of Northern Ireland's best contralto singers and
lead to a successful career in music.

As children at school Alec and Isobel were frequently called
upon to sing the leading parts of some of the traditional ditties
while the rest of the school choir joined in on the chorus.

Alec would sing, "Where are you going to my pretty maid,
I unto her did say..." Then school choir joined in the chorus,
"Heave away, heave away..." Isabel would respond, "I'm going
a-milking kind sir, she said..." They enjoyed these school
programmes.

Mrs. McCarroll, Alec's mother, worked in the reeling room at the local Lindsay Thompson Spinning Mill on Flax Street. Just after the end of the war, her friend at the Mill, Miss Effie Martin, invited Mrs. McCarroll to the Woodvale Mission Hall where Herbie Martin had been appointed as the Missionary by the Woodvale Presbyterian Church. After attending the meetings at the Woodvale Mission Hall for several weeks Mrs. McCarroll became greatly concerned about her spiritual condition and that of her family. As a result of this concern she was converted to Jesus Christ The transformation in Mrs. McCarroll's life was radical and genuine. She found lasting peace in knowing her sins were forgiven and discovered a happiness that would carry her through some of the hard and meagre years that lay ahead.

Mr. McCarroll was greatly handicapped with tuberculosis which was an all too common affliction at that time. This sickness took Mr. McCaroll's life prematurely leaving his wife with three children: Maureen, Alec and Ann. When Mrs. McCarroll saw her husband sinking because of the virulent illness she invited Mr. Martin, the missionary from the Hall, to visit her home and speak to her husband of the importance and necessity of salvation through Jesus Christ. The missionary led Alec's sick dad to personal faith in the Saviour.

Soon after his father's death Alec acquired his first job as a "message boy" at Reeves Cash and Carry Stores just off the Crumlin Road. Besides weighing potatoes on the large cast iron balance-scale he also had to pedal a heavy message-bicycle which had a large and deep basket at the front. This basket was filled with groceries purchased by Mr. Reeves' clients, and Alec had to deliver the goods to their homes.

Pedalling a bicycle laden down with a basket full of groceries was hard work for a slight young lad like Alec. It was even more difficult when he had to deliver the orders to some customers who lived in Ligoniel which was situated several miles farther up the steep Crumlin Road on the lower slopes of the Black Mountain. Perhaps the huffing and puffing of those long bicycle rides helped young Alec develop a good pair of healthy lungs which would enable him to hold on to the high musical notes in future years.

One memory which still lingers with embarrassment on Alec's mind was the day some chocolate biscuits were brought into Reeves Cash & Carry Stores. The post-war years were marked by the rigid use of ration books when no luxury goods were available and only the basic essentials occupied the shop's shelves. The arrival of these new biscuits was quite a novelty and not many packets were available to the general public. Alec covetously eyed the biscuits several times and had a great desire to taste them but realised that this was forbidden. The biscuits were the property of Mr. Reeves, but Alec could resist the temptation no longer. When he thought no one was looking he delved into the bag and took a delectable chocolate biscuit. He was standing there openly enjoying and munching the biscuit when, suddenly and unexpectedly, Mr. Reeves appeared on the scene. Alec nearly choked as he stuffed the rest of the biscuit into his already full mouth. His face turned flaming red with embarrassment. He wished the ground would open under him. He was keenly aware of his guilt. Perhaps it is significant that Alec was converted shortly after this incident when he firmly learned the old Bible truth, "Be sure your sins will find you out."

As well as enjoying the meetings at the Woodvale Mission Hall, Mrs. McCarroll was also anxious to bring her children and friends to know her Saviour too. Alec's Sunday School teacher, Peggy McClean, invited all her pupils to attend the Sunday evening evangelistic service at the mission hall. On the night Alec attended the Immanuel Male Voice Choir had been invited to conduct the service. After singing, testifying and preaching the gospel, a choir member extended an invitation to the unconverted to come to Jesus Christ. The only boy who responded to the invitation and received the Lord Jesus Christ that night was young Alec McCarroll.

Alec's conversion, obviously unplanned by man, would later be recognised as a token of the providence of God in future plans. George Whitely, a member of the Immanuel Choir, took part in the meeting that night. George did not know how much his life would be allied to that of the young lad who trusted the Saviour that night at the Woodvale Mission Hall.

At his mother's instigation Alec secured a job at the Lindsay Thompson Spinning Mill and worked with her in the reeling room, the cleanest part of the mill. Although this move immediately increased Alec's weekly earnings his mother was very insistent that when he became sixteen years old her son should learn a trade.

Just over a year after starting in the mill an opportunity came for Alec to apply for an apprenticeship as a joiner in the carpentry shop at Harland and Wolff Shipyard. This move was to set a pattern for the rest of Alec's life. He applied, was accepted and completed his apprenticeship which developed his carpentry skills. In later years Alec attended various courses and gained appropriate certificates and diplomas which opened the way for him to become a teacher at the Carpentry Department at Larne Technical College, a position he held until his retirement from teaching in 1996.

However, while Alec insists that he owed both his career in music and education to his mother, he is the first to acknowledge that the greatest influence she had on his life, and consequently on that of the Woodvale Quintet, was to invite him to the Woodvale Mission.

Alec and Harry maintained the friendship they had forged as boys and followed the same professional careers. Their mutual interest in soccer bonded that companionship as they played football for some local teams and when possible they attended the major Irish League games. Alec graduated from kicking a football in the streets and in the local Woodvale Park and went on to play soccer semi-professionally in the Irish League and was signed to play outside-left for Larne, Cliftonville and Portadown.

Often Alec and Harry visited each other's homes where their families took an interest in their diverse pastimes. Harry now lived in Palmer Street and Alec was still in Montreal Street. On one of these visits to the McCarroll home Alec's mum, ever keen to win others for the Saviour, invited Harry to attend the Sunday evening service at the Woodvale Mission. Like Alec just a few months previously, Harry also realised his need of salvation in Jesus Christ, and Mr. Martin led him to the Lord Jesus.

After their conversion the boys threw themselves whole heartedly into the work of the Woodvale Mission Hall. Besides attending the Sunday and mid-week meetings they were active in various outreach activities. The night following Alec's conversion he was asked to distribute tracts in his home district. This led to regular tract distribution and involvement in the Saturday and Sunday open-air meetings on the Shankhill and Crumlin Roads. Soon the two boys were each teaching a Sunday School class. On Thursday evenings Alec led the children's meeting when scores of children were packed into the Hall. Their circle of friends began to widen as other young people joined the Hall. Their lives were happy and full. With full-time employment, their pastime in sport and commitment to the programme at the Woodvale Mission, there was little spare time and serving the Lord had become their primary goal.

Alec was greatly helped in his Christian life at work during the lunch hour Bible Study and prayer meetings. Stalwarts like Billy Lavery of the Christian Brethren, Dick Magill, John Andrews and Sammy Rea, taught the Scriptures to the young converts. After quickly digesting a few sandwiches from his lunch box and downing a billie-can of tea at the work bench, Alec joined other workers either down at the far end of the Machine Shop, or if a ship was already on the slips, they met in one of its cabins. The meetings left a lasting impression on young Alec.

Due to the testimony of these men many others came to know the Lord also. One man related that the sight of young Alec McCarroll carrying his New Testament was a rebuke to him as a young apprentice. While Alec and others went to study the Word of God he had his hands full of playing cards as he engaged in a game of poker. Pummelled with guilt because of his fixation with gambling, the young man could not get away from the early impression Alec had made on his life. Subsequently he came to know the Saviour also.

Although Mr. Herbie Martin was the missionary at the Woodvale Mission Hall he did not do all the preaching. That responsibility was accorded to a diversity of preachers and male voice choirs. Some of these choirs were the Ravenhill Male Voice Choir, the Immanuel Male Choir, the Castlereagh Testimony Choir and the Victoria Male Voice Choir, to name but a few. When these large choirs came to conduct a special meeting, for example, the Harvest Thanksgiving Service, the Woodvale Mission Hall was packed to capacity. The atmosphere was dynamic; the singing was rapturous and the meeting was most enjoyable. Harry and Alec sat enchanted and elated to listen to their favourite hymns being sung.

The one group the boys admired most of all was the Donegall Road Singers. Often after the meeting Jock

McCormick and his friends would stay to sing an extra few quartet pieces. Among their favourite songs at that time was, *Give the World a Smile*. Alec and Harry not only admired them, but frequently they tried to emulate the Donegall Road Singers and sing the different vocal parts.

Just about this time Alec and Harry's former school friends, Andy Taggart and John Adams, were also converted. Although Andy had been heavily and seriously involved in sports, he had always been an upright and religious person, regularly attending St. Mary's Church of Ireland on the Crumlin Road. One day when he was walking up the Crumlin Road he noticed a text on a wayside pulpit which just happened to be on the site of the very same church young Alec McCarroll saw burned to the ground during the War. "Jesus said, Ye must be born again," read the text. The gospel verse on the wall of the newly rebuilt-Church made an impact on Andy who decided to inquire more about the meaning of the new birth. As a result of that pursuit, Andy Taggart, in his own home, accepted the Lord Jesus Christ as his Saviour and experienced the new birth for himself. His life was forever changed.

Like his friend, Andy, John Adams was also converted at home. He had listened to the gospel and knew he needed to be saved but had resisted for some time. This resistance became rebellion and John often told how on the night before his conversion he had a rage against God and tore up his Bible and burned it. Graciously, the Lord continued to speak to John until he dissolved in tears, and at his own bedside he asked the Lord Jesus into his heart to be his Saviour. John, like Alec, soon left the employment of the spinning mill for a new job with the British Oxygen Company.

After their conversion John and Andy started to attend the Welcome Hall on Cambrai Street where Mr. Johnson was the superintendent. However, after several months the two lads got restless feet and began to frequent other places of worship. Finally, they settled in the Woodvale Mission where the old camaraderie with Alec and Harry was renewed.

One night after a choir had visited the Woodvale Mission, the four boys and a few others stayed on at the hall to enjoy each other's company around the old stove. Besides exchanging news they sang some of their favourite hymns. It wasn't until then that the four lads realised they had four natural voices for the four parts in a quartet: Alec sang tenor; Harry was baritone; Andy was second tenor and John sang bass. It was more than a striking coincidence that all four lads were the same age, of same slender build, all relatively small in stature and that they were able to combine their voices to make such a pleasant sound.

That night they began by singing, *I Hear Thy Welcome Voice*. The sound was remarkable and those present complimented the boys. With such reassurance they ventured to sing some more hymns such as, *Who can Cheer the Heart like Jesus*. After a while it dawned on them and the others present that they actually had a natural four part harmony.

Little did they know but that from that embryonic group the Woodvale Quintet was born.

> Who can cheer the heart like Jesus,
>   By His presence all divine?
> True and tender, pure and precious,
>   O how blest to call Him mine!
>
> *All that thrills my soul is Jesus;*
> *He is more than life to me; (to me;)*
> *And the fairest of ten thousand,*
>   *In my blessed Lord I see.*

Love of Christ so freely given,
Grace of God beyond degree,
Mercy higher than the heaven,
Deeper than the deepest sea.

What a wonderful redemption,
Never can a mortal know
How my sin, tho' red like crimson,
Can be whiter than the snow.

Every need His hand supplying,
Every good in Him I see;
On His strength divine relying,
He is all in all to me.

By the crystal flowing river
With the ransomed I shall sing,
And for ever and for ever
Praise and glorify the King.

CHAPTER THREE

The Old Fashioned Meeting

❖

HERBIE MARTIN, THE MISSIONARY AT THE WOODVALE MISSION, WAS DELIGHTED TO LEARN that four keen young men from the Woodvale Mission had discovered their musical talent. It was just what was needed at the hall, and Mr. Martin wasted no time inviting them to sing at the Sunday evening service. A lot of practice around the hall's old furnace went into that first public engagement.

The night went well. They sang their two well drilled pieces, *I Hear Thy Welcome Voice* and *Who Can Cheer the Heart Like Jesus.* The hymns were well received by all and afterwards there were plenty of compliments. Mr. Martin was pleased and told the boys to be ready to sing the following week at the open air meeting at the corner of Disraeli Street.

Little by little their confidence grew. More and more they were invited to take part in meetings and special occasions at the Woodvale Mission Hall. With each engagement their harmony and tone seemed to improve. Soon news of their success filtered out beyond the confines of the Woodvale Mission. The name of the group seemed to be an obvious choice - the Woodvale Quartet.

Sammy McGarry, who worked in the Engine Works at Harland and Wolff, was a regular contributor at the shipyard Bible study and prayer meeting. Sammy also led the work in the Bethel Mission Hall at Whitewell on the Belfast's Shore Road. When he heard about the young men and their singing talent he invited them to sing at his weekly open-air meeting in North Belfast. The boys accepted the invitation with a measure of apprehension.

The area around the LMS Railway Station at the end of York Street was teeming with people on that cold but dry Saturday night. Families were returning from their shopping and they mingled with passengers carrying luggage as they streamed in and out of the nearby Railway Station. Sammy McGarry strategically positioned his faithful band of workers in a semi-circle on the opposite side of the road near to the junction of Duncairn Gardens.

After a few rousing hymns Sammy introduced the four young men. Nervously they fumbled with their music sheets. The lighting was inadequate so they had to use a small torch. Even as they pitched their voices for the first notes, the vapour from their exhaling breath indicated the sharp chill in the air. Notwithstanding the dim light and frosty air, the newly formed quartet sang out the gospel with all the sweetness and sincerity they could muster. Their melodious tones rang out on the night air as again they sang *Who Can Cheer the Heart Like Jesus*. Christian workers from the Bethel Mission distributed gospel literature. From the middle of the semi-circle a few short testimonies were presented to the passers-by. Others stepped forward to the centre of the group and called out appropriate

Bible texts. Again the four lads were invited to sing. They clustered together around the centre of the circle with the torch focused on the music. They rendered their arrangement of *I Hear Thy Welcome Voice that Calls Me Now to Thee*. Various people stopped on both sides of York Street to listen to these four young men not knowing that they were taking their first steps in a long musical career. When the four returned to their more familiar surroundings on the Crumlin Road there was a measure of satisfaction that for the first time they had served their Lord beyond the walls of the Woodvale Mission.

Soon invitations began to accumulate for the newly formed quartet to sing at mission halls and churches in the Shankhill and Crumlin Roads areas. As these invitations increased the boys had to increase their repertoire and give more time practicing and developing their arrangements. They also tried to safeguard their contribution to the Woodvale Mission and therefore made a ruling to keep the first Sunday of each month free so that they could retain close links with their home fellowship.

Other Christian quartets were also very active in gospel witness in Belfast at that time - the Iron Hall Quartet, the Victoria Quartet, the Belmont Quartet, the Crystal River Quartet and the Living Waters Quartet were all kept busy in singing the gospel around Northern Ireland. This reflects a measure of the spiritual temperature and evangelistic thrust of that time. Even though all these groups had a full diary of engagements, there was still plenty of room for the new boys on the block - the Woodvale Quartet.

The increased demand for their talents began to squeeze their leisure activities. There was not just so much time for football and other pursuits, but they became aware of and made time for several Christian girls.

Alec showed a lot of interest in a young girl from Oldpark Presbyterian Church. Jean Beattie was a very keen Christian who worked in the Faulat Shirt Factory in Agnes Street. Like Alec at the shipyard, she also found great help from other Christian girls at lunch hour when they had times of fellowship. Their romance blossomed, and in a short time Jean became an enthusiastic supporter of the Woodvale Quartet.

About that time Harry Yates had been introduced to Jean's cousin, Meta French from Manor Street, and they also started to go out with each other. Andy had met Belle Allen who was also from Oregan Street, and soon he was paying her a lot of attention. These three members of the group married their sweethearts and consequently they nearly doubled their number as each introduced his wife to a non-singing role of the Woodvale Quartet fraternity. Encouraged by the men, the three ladies also formed a musical trio and sang in various meetings. It wasn't until some years later that John Adams met a young girl whom he married, and they settled in Dublin.

As their experience increased the four fellows in the Woodvale Quartet not only made their musical contribution to a meeting but they were also able to conduct the full service. They testified and sang, but John and Harry seemed to be the most gifted preachers among them and publicly handled the Scriptures. After the first year of the Quartet's ministry, it was John's aptitude for preaching that presented the first major hurdle for the Woodvale.

John Adams was a very conscientious student of God's Word, and he was a maturing preacher. Apart from preaching periodically for the Quartet, he and Andy were also invited to speak for the Rev. Henry at the John White Congregational Church near John's home in Oregan Street. He also had opportunity to help in the work of the Immanuel Mission in Wellwood Street near Sandy Row.

John's involvement in Christian work created a growing desire to give his life to the ministry of the Word of God. After four years of ministry with the quartet and through his involvement at the Immanuel Mission, John came into contact with a like-minded brother in the Lord, Jimmy Hughes. Both men expressed their aspiration to serve the Lord in the needy areas of the South of Ireland. John's departure was half expected, but it still came as a shock when he announced that he was leaving the Woodvale Quartet.

Although Jimmy Hughes and John engaged in open-air ministry in the South of Ireland for eighteen months, later they followed separate paths. John remained in the South of Ireland to pursue his ministry in the Dublin area where he resumed employment with the British Oxygen Company. He returned to Belfast to marry Lily Coulter from Shankhill Baptist, and they returned to set up their home in Ireland's Fair City. They were very happy in Dublin and were blessed with two children, Dave and Elizabeth Anne. Sadly, Belle died of cancer while yet a young woman. John later met and married a daughter of a well known Christian businessman, Mr. Reggie Squires, and became involved in their family business. He settled in the fellowship at Northumberland Hall and today, in spite of ill health, he is an elder in the Evangelical Church in Dunloaghrie.

John's imminent departure set the other three lads praying to find a suitable replacement. It was then that they learned that Victor Agnew was available to step into John's place. Victor, who belonged to Derg Street City Mission, besides being a very talented bass singer, was also a very gifted preacher to both children and adults. On special occasions he enthralled the children with his graphic illustrations of Bible stories and Scripture lessons which he drew on a chalkboard. This added a new dimension to the quartet's ministry.

Just when the quartet was satisfied that one problem had been solved and Victor Agnew seemed to be a suitable replacement for John Adams, they then faced another major obstacle which threatened the future of the quartet.

On Sunday mornings Andy Taggart attended John White Memorial Congregational Church. The Rev. J. N. Henry, the minister of the church who had given preaching opportunities to John Adams, heard of Andy's growing competence in the pulpit and invited him to speak at a few mid-week meetings when the minister was absent. At these meetings Andy and Alec sang duets and led the congregation in community singing. Andy then preached a short message.

One night Mr. Henry said he had heard good reports about Andy's speaking and suggested he might consider applying for the Congregational ministry. Andy was startled at the suggestion. At first Andy thought it would be highly improbable because he had no academic qualifications that would admit him to a college. However, after much prayer and some gentle persuasion, Andy realised the Congregational ministry was God's will for his life.

Alec and Harry Yates were confounded when they heard the news. Their first reaction was to think of the future of the quartet having lost John Adams what would they now do without Andy? Where would they find a second tenor? However, Andy was convinced this was God's call to him. The confirmation to this call came when he passed the entrance exams to Paton College, the Congregational Theological College in Nottingham.

Andy soon left home to pursue his new calling. He never returned to live in Northern Ireland again except for occasional visits to his family and friends. During the four years Andy studied at Paton College he had the opportunity to be pastor of Lenton Baptist Church in Nottingham. While there in his new position Andy took the opportunity to introduce the quartet to the Nottingham church for their annual Easter convention.

The weekends the quartet spent in Nottingham were very full and tiring. However, the fellowship was tremendous and the Lord blessed their ministry. Finally, after his graduation from Paton College, Andy followed his vocation to pastor a Congregational Church near Manchester.

Just about the same time Andy left for England, Alec and Jean were married and set up home in Ballysillan, farther up the North Belfast mountain slope. Because of Alec and Jean's wedding and Andy's departure, the Quartet eased off on the number of engagements. They earnestly prayed that God would guide them about a replacement for Andy so their musical ministry could continue. Andy's vacancy marked the start of an unsettled period in the history of the Quartet.

Attention turned to Eric Burns, a talented painist who also had a rich tenor voice. His wife, Maureen, worked with Jean McCarroll, Alec's wife; and both were stitchers in the Faulat Shirt Factory on Agnes Street. They were also close friends at Oldpark Presbyterian Church.

When Eric was approached to consider singing second tenor with the Woodvale, he felt this was an opportunity to serve the Lord. The quartet was complete again and arrangements were made to resume a full programme of engagements. This did not last long because just after Eric joined the group, he had a career change from being a bread server for a local bakery to an officer at the Rathgael Corrective Home in Bangor. Before taking up his new position he had to study for a period in England and therefore, after a short career with the Woodvale Quartet, he reluctantly relinquished his involvement with his colleagues. Presently Eric is an elder in Rathcoole Presbyterian Church and still keeps close contact with the Woodvale.

The disappointment of Eric's premature exit gave urgency to finding another second tenor. Angus Burton was the answer to this pursuit. Angus who came from the Ormeau Road sang second tenor as part of Victoria Quartet for several years. This group was based at Great Victoria Street Baptist Church. Due to their numbers being depleted when Tom Stacey, one of their leading members, emigrated, they decided to disband. This left Angus available and when approached, he readily consented to sing with the Woodvale.

Back in those early and formative years of the Quartet none of the members had a car. They all depended on public transport both for travelling to and from the practices after their day's work as well as travelling to various meetings in the city and beyond. It is almost unimaginable now what it must have been like then not to have the convenience of door to door transport to those distant meetings in remote parts of Ulster. However, the great joy in serving the Lord Jesus and singing for Him far outweighed any inconvenience and was not looked upon as sacrifice.

No sooner had Angus joined the Quintet than Victor Agnew, who had made a big contribution to their ministry for a few years, stepped down. He emigrated from Northern Ireland to live in Canada, and his departure created another big gap. His was not an easy role to fill. Victor's responsibilities apart from singing bass included preaching, ministering through chalkboard illustrations and planning all the bookings for the group.

Victor's unexpected departure from the group disguised some tremendous blessings the Lord had in store for the Quartet. One day Alec was unpacking boxes in his new Ballysillan home when he noticed a friend, John Gardiner, strolling through the new development approaching his home. John had been a member of the Living Waters Quartet. His father had been a very keen Christian and eager soul winner and at their family home in Charlieville Street Mr. Gardiner often held cottage meetings. To make room for neighbouring friends who attended these meetings Mr. Gardiner had to remove all the furniture and rearrange the house. People crammed into the house each week to hear the gospel. Mr. Gardiner was enthusiastic to win his neighbours for the Lord, but his greatest satisfaction was leading his own family to the Saviour. Alec welcomed John to his home. After preliminary greetings John intimated he had come see Alec about a particular matter the need of a second bass in the quartet.

He had heard of the vacancy from Alec's sister Maureen at Jersey Street Mission Hall the previous night. John had a good quality low toned voice and great versatility with music. John told Alec that he felt the Lord had put it in his heart to offer himself to the Woodvale Quartet.

Alec was overwhelmed with joy and admiration at John's offer. The members of the quartet had been praying that God would send a suitable replacement for Victor Agnew. To have found someone with such considerable talents and remarkable Christian character was a God send. Alec mentioned to the other quartet members about John's approach and conversation, and they all agreed that John Gardiner was an unmistakable answer to their prayers. John's thirty-five years of service with the Woodvale until his sudden death in May 1993 was eloquent evidence of his devoted commitment to the Quartet and to His Lord. Only eternity will disclose how great was the impact of the work and witness of this godly and talented man.

Besides attending the Woodvale Mission Hall when possible, Alec also worshipped at the Mustard Seed Mission Hall on Sunday mornings while his wife, Jean, continued to attend Oldpark Presbyterian Church. Having been associated with both the Woodvale and Mustard Seed Halls since his conversion, Alec felt that both he and Jean needed to be identified with a church in the area. After much prayer and heart searching they were both baptised by immersion. Subsequently they applied and were accepted as members of Cliftonpark Avenue Baptist Church. This step would bring the Woodvale Quartet into a wider involvement with other people who yet would have meaningful roles to play in the continuance of the Woodvale's musical ministry.

After a few years with a continuous and settled group of four regular members the quartet again hit on troubled times. Angus Burton found it was increasingly difficult to handle both his singing commitments and his secular obligations. He had been promoted at work, and his added responsibilities put extra demands on his time. As a consequence he had to step down from the Quartet. This again created a vacancy that disrupted the continuity of the Woodvale's ministry.

Unknown to the group, the Lord had another singer waiting in the wings who would also make a very valuable contribution to the development of the quartet's sound. Billy Ennis like John Gardiner had been a member of the Living Waters Quartet and had previously sung with the accomplished Golden City Quartet. Billy was a local fellow of the same age group as the original Woodvale Quartet members and lived near to the John White Memorial Congregational Church. His past experience in gospel singing allowed him to not only slot in easily to the group, but he was also able to bring with him many new revolutionary concepts that helped give a new dimension to the Woodvale's harmonious sound. Billy Ennis was an innovator. He was not only gifted in playing the guitar but was also a versatile vocalist. His range of voice allowed him to sing any part. He radically changed the quartet's whole approach to singing. Up until then they had been singing traditional male voice choir pieces which were well known, but these tended to limit the quartet's scope. It didn't give them any distinctive features and until Billy changed their whole approach to gospel singing they had just been another quartet.

Billy brought in a range of new pieces which he obtained from some of the great gospel quartets in the United States. He also introduced the use of a lead singer, a role which he fulfilled with excellent results. He was the first to suggest a gradual build up of the volume of voice and then a change of key. This added great effect and emphasis to the message they sang about. Although Billy was a competent guitarist he seldom used the instrument as backing music. He much preferred acapello singing to allow an appreciation for the rich vocal sounds using the guitar only to give the initial key. These procedures are very acceptable and familiar with present day singing groups, but at that time they were quite revolutionary.

Just as these new techniques were being initiated the group was invited to sing at the Bangor Missionary Convention. Marie Crawford, the accomplished organist for all the convention meetings, approached the group and commended them for their new sound. She said she could hardly believe it was the same Woodvale she had heard before, and said they had shown a lot of courage to break the traditional mold and make a departure from going round in an orbit of the well known and well worn male choir pieces. With that encouragement the Quintet never returned to the old pattern and well worn singing style.

The influence of the Quartet's ministry and God's blessing upon them was manifested in many ways. Christians were greatly blessed, and others were saved. This was a great encouragement to their ministry. However, because of various outside factors and demands on the member's time, there was a continuing difficulty within the Quartet to retain a full quota of singers for any considerable period of time. More permanent members who could be committed to the ministry were needed. This was a regular and ongoing matter for prayer.

In 1965 George Whitely arrived as an answer to those prayers. His admission into the quartet arose from a characteristically amusing incident, and yet it marked an important milestone. John Gardiner was seemingly indispensable to the Quartet as he had not only fully integrated as part of the team, but his contribution greatly enriched the range and balance of the Quartet's sound. One night the group were booked to sing and speak at Rathcoole Baptist Church when seeming calamity struck. John had arrived late that afternoon to say he had been to the dentist to receive a new set of dentures and they didn't feel comfortable. In the local vernacular of the time John summed it up, "I think the dentist has fixed me up with a Devon grate instead of a set of false teeth." It was not only difficult for him to speak and eat but there was definitely no way he could sing.

In their dilemma the boys remembered that "big" George Whitely had recently relinquished his position with Immanuel Male Voice Choir which meant he was free. He and Sadie were also members at Cliftonpark Avenue Baptist and lived in the immediate vicinity. For many years George, who was a glazier by trade, sang in the choir and also ministered the Word of God. He always felt an attachment with Alec and the original group as he was a member the Immanuel Male Voice Choir which conducted the meeting the night of Alec's conversion in the old Woodvale Mission Hall. When George was approached to help out in the emergency he was only too willing to accommodate the Quartet in their predicament.

Big George was an immediate favourite that night at Rathcoole Baptist. When they sang *Would You Be Free From Your Burden of Sin,* he characteristically added many repetitive and varied little extras at the end of each verse. The evening was such an immense success that George was instantly invited to remain as a permanent member of the group. When John eventually got used to his new set of teeth he rejoined the group and the Woodvale Quartet was expanded to become the Woodvale Quintet.

Requests coming from churches and mission halls, small meetings and large gatherings, for the Quintet to sing and speak were increasing. The new sound was most appealing and greatly welcomed by all. As well as singing all over Ulster and having the joy of bringing blessing and comfort to many, they also had the personal joy and satisfaction of winning people to the Lord Jesus Christ.

Their old friend Andy Taggart who had graduated from college and been called to a Congregational Church near Manchester, invited his old companions over to conduct a special weekend of meetings at his new church. This trip to England opened many opportunities for the Quintet to sing in England and Scotland. There was great joy amongst the five fellows and their wives in serving the Lord.

Just when it seemed that the Woodvale Quintet had a good settled group, Alec's life long friend from school, Harry Yates, felt it was time for him to disengage from singing with the group. Harry had not only been with the them from its inception, but he was the main preacher at their meetings. For Harry to leave the group was going to be a huge loss, but he was studying for his Higher National Certificate exams at work and felt he had to give more time to study and concentrate on these as singing in a quartet involved a lot of practice nights. After some negotiations Harry consented to continue preaching for the Quartet and yield his musical role to a replacement. It was now back to the drawing board for the singers and back to prayer to ask for God's guidance for the right musical replacement for Harry. Again this change proved to mark a significant chapter in the history of the Woodvale Quintet. Throughout these changes the Quintet continued to sing and preach the same unchanging gospel at every opportunity they were given.

'Twas an old fashioned meeting,
In an old fashioned place,
That some old fashioned people,
Found some old fashioned grace.
As an old fashioned sinner, I began to pray,
And God heard me and saved me,
In the old fashioned way.

I love that singing camp-meeting style,
It makes me happy, it makes me smile.
When you love your fellow man,
And that feeling's mighty grand,
When you're singing camp-meeting style.

Give me that old-time religion,
Give me that old-time religion,
Give me that old-time religion,
It's good enough for me.

It was good for Paul and Silas,
It was good for Paul and Silas,
It was good for Paul and Silas,
It's good enough for me.

CHAPTER FOUR

Through It All

❖

JACK BRADLEY, A LIVERPUDLIAN AND FORMER
MISSIONARY WITH THE SUDAN INTERIOR
Mission in Africa, was the pastor at Cliftonpark Avenue Baptist
Church. Under his leadership the church purchased two houses
which were adjacent to the church property. In these renovated
premises he introduced an all-age Sunday School which
convened one hour earlier than the morning service. This
pioneer venture in Northern Ireland was an immense success
initially and attracted many new visitors and members to the
church.

One Sunday morning just about the time Alec McCarroll
was hanging his coat in the church cloakroom, he met a visitor
to the church. He recognised him as Roy Melville, the brother
of Tommy Melville, with whom Alec had worked in the Belfast
shipyard. Roy had come with Joan Stockman, his fiancé, to
Cliftonpark Avenue Baptist Church at the invitation of Sam

Best, as they were looking for a new spiritual home. Both Roy and Joan were pleased to meet someone else they knew.

Roy had been reared in the Tiger's Bay area of Belfast and was employed as a travelling salesman for J. C. Brow's, an agency for catering equipment at Prince Regent Road in Belfast. Through his work Roy made many friends all over Northern Ireland. Later he left J. C. Brows when he was presented with the opportunity to buy a small fruit and vegetable shop on North Queen Street near Duncairn Gardens.

Since his youth Roy had chummed around with Sam Best, George Magilton, Jim Shaw and Davey Spence all of whom came from the same general North Belfast area. All these young men were converted at special evangelistic meetings convened at the North Belfast Mission where Rev. John Fleming and Rev. John Keyes had been preaching. Each of these young men later made a great Christian impact, and a few of them developed considerable preaching ability. However, all of them would admit that none made more spiritual impact than Roy Melville.

Roy married Joan at the North Belfast Mission which had been their spiritual home since their conversion, but once they set up their new home they settled into the church family at Cliftonpark Avenue Baptist. Roy soon became actively involved in the work and outreach of the church. He not only had a Sunday School class but was also engaged in door-to-door visitation and open-air witness in the greater area. Within a few years Roy was elected to be a deacon in the church. He never missed a meeting except for sickness or circumstances that made his presence impossible.

Roy not only was a dedicated and zealous Christian worker but also had a beautiful, rich and velvety baritone voice. Those who sat near him in church could not help but hear Roy when he sang the congregational hymns. Recognising his own talent

Roy sought to put it to good use and accepted many invitations to sing solos at various church meetings in Belfast.

The people at Cliftonpark Avenue Church, recognising this evident gift, promptly made recommendations to the Quintet to make use of Roy Melville in their ministry. This suggestion dovetailed with Harry Yates' position of adopting a preaching role and allowed his singing part to be given to another. In Harry's absence Roy was invited to blend his baritone voice and become a lead singer with the Quintet - all this was in accord with Billy Ennis' plans and new approach to Quintet singing. When the invitation was put to Roy, he responded favourably and soon was integrated into the group.

This discovery was an immediate success. Roy, who stood over six feet tall, had great composure and confidence as he sang and had the ability to make the congregation relax as he sweetly, but sincerely, sang out the gospel. He often sang the lead part, while on other occasions he blended his voice with the Quintet. No matter whether Roy sang one of the new hymns or an old gospel song, he had the ability to always make it a memorable occasion.

The first time Roy sang with the Quintet was at the Iron Hall in East Belfast. For those present it was an unforgettable experience. On that night the Quintet decided to sing an old piece, *Redeemed How I Love To Proclaim It*. As previously arranged by Billy Ennis, Roy took the lead in singing the verses, and the other voices combined to support him on the chorus. People from the Iron Hall enquired from Alec and the other members where they had found this fellow with such a voice. The people were not only blessed, they were amazed at the ease and warmth with which Roy sang. In the after-meeting that followed on that Sunday night the group sang a few more pieces, and with great effect Roy again took the lead to sing, *In Times Like These We Need a Saviour.*

Roy was very much Billy's prodigy who encouraged and taught him new approaches to his music for better effect. His imposing height made Roy stand head and shoulders above his singing colleagues. On occasions when the others might have been nervous about having to sing before great crowds, Roy, with apparent natural serenity, stepped forward and sang in an inspiring way. Some well-intentioned people advised that Roy should have his voice trained professionally so that he could give better expression in his voice. They were convinced he had a professional future in Christian music.

All those who heard Roy will never forget when he sang *The Stranger of Galilee:*

> The Sands have been washed in the footprints
> Of the Stranger of Galilee's shore.
> And the voice that subdued the rough billows,
> Will be heard in Judea no more.

> And I felt I could love Him forever
> So tender and precious was He
> I claimed that day as my Saviour
> The Stranger of Galilee

Even as he sang, one's imagination seemed to drift off to that distant Galilean coast and could almost sense the lapping of the waves at the water's edge as Roy's mellow voice sang of His Saviour. He articulated the words with such meaning and expression that it made the biblical scene come to life. When he repeated the chorus, "And I felt I could love Him forever" it seemed as if everyone in the service wanted to join in with a sincere, but an emotional outburst of impulsive love for the Lord Jesus Christ.

On one particular Saturday the Woodvale Quintet was invited to participate in the afternoon and evening meetings at a special Bible conference at Armagh Baptist Church by Pastor James Armstrong. After the evening meeting they travelled from Ireland's ecclesiastical capital to Lurgan Baptist Church where they were to be guests at a Festival of Male Voice Praise. En route to Lurgan Billy Ennis dropped a bombshell and shocked the lads to a stunned silence. Billy announced that he and his family had decided to emigrate to Canada. At the time many other Ulster folk had taken a similar step and there was constant drain of people looking for a better life-style for their families. Billy explained that he and his wife felt it was the right step for them. No one could answer or protest such a decision. He intimated that his departure would not be for another few months but suggested they look out for a second tenor to replace him.

To find a replacement for Billy Ennis would be a formidable if not an impossible assignment. Through Billy's influence the Quintet had not only developed better sound but they had also grown in the public's estimation of their quality and competence. To find a singer to replace Billy Ennis would not be easy, but they felt it would be impossible to replace him as an arranger of their music.

The Lord had His plans for the Quintet. In the fraternity among gospel singing groups which operated in Northern Ireland, several singers emerged with considerable distinction. One of these was Denis Kennedy who for thirteen years had been singing with a quartet from his own church - the Ulster Temple Quintet. Denis was reared in a Christian home. Mr. Kennedy, his dad, dedicated a lot of his time showing Trinity evangelistic films all around Belfast. Denis not only accompanied his Dad but became quite skilful in setting up the projector and equipment for showing the film. One night at the Wellington Hall in central Belfast Mr. Kennedy showed a movie. At the close of the meeting an appeal was made for those who would come to Jesus Christ. Much to the surprise of Mr. Kennedy his young son, Denis, walked the aisle that night - a mother and father's prayers were answered.

Often the paths of these singing groups would cross, and one group would hear the other sing at various venues. Just when Billy Ennis announced his plan to emigrate it was learned that the Ulster Temple Quintet had suffered a similar setback. Their tenor, Willie Weir, had already left Ulster to live in Canada, and as a result of his departure the Ulster Temple Quintet had ceased to exist. The dissolution of the Quintet left Denis Kennedy free from singing engagements, although he was heavily involved in the work of his church in East Belfast.

The Woodvale was invited to sing at a special service in the Branagh Mission in East Belfast. During the meeting they noticed Denis Kennedy and his dad sitting in the congregation. Alec McCarroll suggested that perhaps an approach could be made to him as a replacement for Billy Ennis; after the meeting when Denis and his dad had gone out to their car and were sitting waiting for a few passengers, Alec went over to the car and greeted them both. He enquired if Denis was presently occupied with any other group, and to this Alec got a reply, "No." He then suggested that Denis should consider joining the ministry of the Woodvale Quartet.

Denis, a tanker driver with Shell Oil, answered, "Tempt me." He told Alec that to sing with the Woodvale Quintet would be the fulfilment of his life's ambition. He had always admired the quality and sound of the Woodvale and had dreamed of the day he could be part of it; but he had never really thought it would ever happen. Denis was gifted with a very smooth, mellow and mature voice. The following week Alec and Roy Melville went to visit Denis and his wife Moira at their

Orangefield home and talked the whole matter over. At the end of the visit both Roy and Alec were convinced that Denis was the person they needed.

Denis' admission to the Quintet in 1969 proved to be another landmark in the meandering story of the Woodvale Quintet. Denis was not a preacher but had a very good voice as a soloist and leading vocalist. He was an ideal replacement for Billy Ennis. Even though Billy left Ulster's shores, he maintained a long and productive association with the Woodvale. For twenty five-years he supplied the Woodvale Quintet with musical material from United States making suggestions about various musical arrangements they could sing.

With Roy Melville and Denis Kennedy as their two quality lead singers the Woodvale's tone and sound were greatly enhanced. Their ability to communicate the gospel in song continued to attract hundreds of people who came to numerous venues to hear them. God blessed their ministry as they not only sang the gospel but testified and preached as opportunity allowed.

At Cliftonpark Avenue Baptist Church a further building progamme was undertaken, and the men of the church worked hard to enlarge their premises. Men and women of the church voluntarily worked hard to build a large room at the rear of the main church building and the newly acquired adjoining houses. Weeks of great fellowship ensued as they worked together on the project. When the new hall was completed Alec was asked to arrange a programme for a special night of song and praise to inaugurate the new extension.

Wanting to put on a programme worthy of the occasion Alec thought of who might make the best contribution for the night. His mind immediately went to Campbell and Margaret Archer from Bangor.

Campbell had been raised in a Christian home. He, however, had not been converted until he was eighteen years old. He was a very accomplished guitar player, and during his time at Orangefield School on Belfast's Castlereagh Road, he had been part of a skiffle pop group which included the celebrated vocalist and musician Van Morrison.

Van and Campbell shared a mutual love for the guitar and spent many hours together plucking strings and rehearsing chords at their Bloomfield homes. However, other pastimes also occupied Campbell's life. It was at a Boy's Brigade Camp in Southport during a typical wet week under canvas that Campbell came to know Jesus Christ as Saviour. The wet weather confined the boys to the camp site, and most of the week was spent singing songs, choruses and hymns.

Unwittingly, through the music and choruses, the gospel was having a great effect on Campbell. All the teaching of former years at Sunday School seemed to fill his heart and mind. Finally, on the last night in the tent Campbell could resist the Saviour no longer. His parents' prayers were answered and Campbell accepted the Lord Jesus on his knees at the side of his camp bed.

After Campbell's conversion he parted ways with Van Morrison who went on to international fame and success in show business. Campbell though, wanted to dedicate his life to the Lord Jesus Christ and was soon active in Christian service. His musical talent was an obvious asset, and this was also greatly enhanced when he married Margaret Sykes in 1966. Margaret was a very gifted singer and from the time she was young she had sung solo at many meetings and evangelistic rallies.

Campbell became part of the Green Pastures Quartet, and for eight years he employed both his musical and vocal competence with the group. Appropriately dressed in green blazers for their engagements they served the Lord in various meetings all over Northern Ireland. When the Green Pastures Quartet finally ceased to operate, Campbell and his wife Margaret combined to form a very acceptable and successful duet ministry. For three years they were in much demand all over the country, but with the arrival of their children this activity had to be curtailed somewhat.

It was the success of this duet ministry that influenced Alec to include Campbell and Margaret on the programme at Clifton Park Avenue Baptist Church. In those days, when not many houses had a telephone, it was initially very difficult to contact Campbell. He was a chauffeur in a limousine service of a leading Northern Ireland industrial company. His work meant he was frequently away from home. Normally when there was difficulty contacting a singer Alec would have thought of someone else more readily accessible and available. However, Alec persisted telephoning from a public call box every day until finally Campbell and Margaret were booked to sing at the praise service for the opening of Cliftonpark's new hall.

This meeting proved to be another turning point in the development of the Woodvale Quintet. Furthermore, the Woodvale took part in the programme that night; Campbell and Margaret also excelled. In conversation over supper afterwards Alec enquired from Campbell what his plans were for the future. Campbell said he was enjoying what they were doing, but he was also missing his previous quartet ministry. Alec suggested the possibility of Campbell playing guitar as backing music for the Woodvale Quintet. At first Campbell thought it was only a tease, but when he realised it was a serious proposition he positively showed his enthusiasm for the opportunity. The other members of the Quintet were consulted on the spot about the Campbell's inclusion and promptly approved.

Until that night at Clifton Park the Woodvale sound had seldom ever been accompanied by any musical instrument.

Their voices had always blended in acappello. However, because of Campbell's skill and dexterity on the guitar, the men were glad to welcome him to the team.

No time was lost that very night. Immediately supper ended the group, accompanied by their new recruit, practised with the guitar in the adjoining church sanctuary. They all felt it was an immediate success. Without further ado Campbell was invited to be part of the Woodvale ministry. One of the great songs of the time summed up the changing times and difficulties the Woodvale had faced:

I've seen many tears and sorrows,
I've had questions for tomorrow,
There've been times when I didn't know right from wrong,
But in every situation, God gave me consolation,
That my trials came to only make me strong.

Through it all, through it all,
I've learned to trust in Jesus,
I've learned to trust in God.
Through it all, through it all,
I've learned to depend upon His Word.

I've been to a lot of places,
And I've seen a lot of faces,
But there were times when I felt so all alone,
But in my lonely hours, yes, those precious lonely hours,
Jesus let me know that I was all His own.

I thank Him for the mountains,
And I thank Him for the for the valleys,
And I thank Him for the storms He brought me through,
If I'd never had a problem, I'd never know that God could solve them,
I'd never know what faith in God can do.

CHAPTER FIVE

Victory In Jesus

---------------------------- ❖ ----------------------------

MUSIC IS NOT A HUMAN INVENTION. BESIDES JEHOVAH SINGING OVER HIS PEOPLE, THE Scriptures remind us that the morning stars sang for joy as God laid the great foundations of the earth. Songs and psalms played a major part of worship both in the Old and New Testaments. Within hours of our Saviour's death He joined His own disciples singing the Passover Hallel. The Apostolic church sang victorious praises in their witness and worship. Singing made a vital contribution in the first conversion of a man in Europe; a jailor in Philippi, who was won for Jesus Christ. Since then the Church has been vocal with sacred song. Augustine wrote of being "made to weep with the hymns and spiritual songs transported by the voices of the congregation sweetly singing" on the occasion of his baptism. Martin Luther's enemies complained that the great reformer had done "more harm by his songs than by his sermons." Reformation martyrs sang their praises to God in a final witness to Jesus

Christ as hot flames leaped around them. Charles Wesley composed more than four thousand hymns in the years of great spiritual awakening in England. Authors such as Isaac Watt, John Newton and Fanny Crosby are only a few of those who have left us a rich heritage of Christian music and song.

Charles M. Alexander said, "I do not recall any religious awakening without gospel singing. Music was a vital partof the revival under the Wesleys. The revival of 1859 was a time of hymn-singing. Gospel songs were half the power of the Moody and Sankey meetings. They began to share meetings in 1874 and soon established the gospel singer and the gospel song as the greatest of all agencies as the winning of souls for Jesus Christ. It is a well known fact that the text, the sermon and the strongest appeals from the pulpit often go unheeded or forgotten, while the song finds an abiding place in the hearts of all hearers" Often it is the music and the song that engages the attention of the hearers and makes their hearts receptive to the message expressed.

The Woodvale's musical ministry was increasingly fruitful even though it had undergone a considerable number of changes of personnel. The latest composition of the Quintet was Alec McCarroll, John Gardiner, Roy Melville, George Whitely, and Dennis Kennedy. Campbell Archer's addition to the Quintet was primarily as musical backing for the other five singers. The auxiliary music backing was hailed everywhere as a great contribution, and the ministry of the Quintet was in greater demand all over the country.

The fellowship among the boys and their wives was very special. Besides meeting at the various church venues they also visited each other's homes. Sometimes their conversation was serious and on other occasions quite hilarious.

Unknown to the Quintet, during those halcyon days of great fellowship and effective ministry, the Lord was silently but surely planning ahead for them. Six months after Campbell started with the Quintet, Roy Melville became ill. Initially it was a surprise to his other colleagues to discover that Roy was unwell as he had always been strong and physically robust. Surprise was to give way to shock when the nature of Roy's illness became clear.

Late in 1972 the Quintet were invited by Pastor Peter Donald to be part of a special week of meetings at John Harper Memorial Baptist Church in Glasgow. Dr. Alan Redpath was the speaker at the meetings. God richly blessed Dr. Redpath's powerful preaching and the musical contributions were excellent. During the same week Roy complained that he felt unwell and that his throat felt a bit raw. He tried to persevere singing but had to opt out one evening due to his worsening condition. Campbell, also a baritone, took Roy's place.

Immediately on his return to Belfast Roy consulted his doctor for the throat complaint. It seemed to be the normal "bad throat," and a "bottle" was duly prescribed for the complaint. However, Roy did not improve. Soon the "bad throat" seemed to cause other difficulties for Roy.

One night all the Quintet members and their wives were at a wedding party in the Lisburn Road home of Mr. Herbie Murray whose daughter Maybeth was soon to be married to George Whitely's son Billy. In the course of conversation that evening Roy shared with George Whitely and Alec and Jean McCarroll that he had encountered increasing difficulty in swallowing. His friends suggested he have a word with Maybeth Murray, the bride to be, as she was a nurse at a cancer clinic in Belfast. Roy explained to Maybeth what he felt, and she recommend that he see his family doctor for there was a possibility he could have a small growth in his digestive system. Roy and Joan were stunned at Maybeth's suspicion. He was so shocked and unnerved he couldn't drive home after supper.

That night seemed very long for Roy and his wife. Early the next day he made immediate contact with his doctor. This second consultation with his General Practitioner confirmed the probability of a tumour and the doctor made an appointment for Roy with a consultant at the Royal Victoria Hospital.

When Roy was examined at the out-patients it was concluded that he should remain in hospital without returning home since his condition was so serious. Roy had been diagnosed as having a malignant growth on the alimentary track. He was only thirty-eight years old and radical surgery had to be done immediately to remove his stomach. Although he was released from hospital several weeks after the operation, Roy never recovered to his former strength.

A short time following his release from hospital Roy accompanied the Quintet to two engagements. One was to Windsor Baptist Church and Roy's last meeting with the Quintet was at East End Baptist Church in Belfast. His gaunt frame and pale colour made Roy appear as only a shadow of his former self, however, his voice was still sweet and mellow.

This would be the last time for him to sing at a public meeting. That night, even though he was so weak, he sang his favourite solo written by the former American Country and Western star, Stuart Hamblin:

> My heart can sing when I pause to remember,
>   A heartache here is but a stepping stone;
>   Along a trail that's winding ever upwards,
>   This troubled world is not my final home,
>
> *But until then my heart will go on singing,*
>   *Until then with joy I'll carry on,*
>   *Until the day my eyes behold the city,*
>   *Until the day God calls me home.*

The things of earth will dim and lose their value,
If we recall they're borrowed for a while;
And things of earth that cause the heart to tremble,
Remembered there will only bring a smile,

This weary world with all its toil and struggle
May take its toll of misery and strife;
The soul of man is like a waiting falcon,
When it's released it's destined for the skies,

How poignant and meaningful were the words of that hymn. It was his favourite. After the meeting Roy sat down and wept for he knew he would not be able to continue with the ministry he had loved so much but had been spared to enjoy for just a few short years. He knew this was to be his last public meeting.

Roy's worsening condition caused him to be admitted soon again to the Royal Victoria Hospital. In spite of the excellent nursing care and valiant medical attention Roy's deterioration was rapid. The Scriptures remind us that "though our outward man perish, yet the inward man is renewed day by day." (2 Corinthians 4:16) Through all the weeks of Roy's severe suffering and physical frailty his bright testimony shone so radiantly. Friends from numerous churches came to visit Roy and assure him and Joan of their thoughts and prayers. All who called went away greatly blessed and touched by Roy's witness in his evident weakness.

In the small side ward provided for him in the Royal Victoria Hospital, Roy could often be heard singing some of his favourite hymns. It was his best way of testifying to his fellow patients and the medical staff of his real and living faith in Jesus Christ. One of the hymns he sang was:

'Tis so sweet to trust in Jesus,
Just to take Him at His Word;
Just to rest upon His promise
Just to know "Thus saith the Lord."

Jesus, Jesus, how I trust Him!
How I've proved Him o'er and o'er!
Jesus, Jesus, precious Jesus!
Oh, for grace to trust Him more.

One day while the Quintet was visiting Roy in hospital they sang some of their better known songs. Both patients and nurses gathered round to listen to the Quintet as Roy tried to accompany them. Roy asked Alec to help prop him up in the bed. Even as Alec put his arm around his frail friend he felt that Roy's emaciated frame was just like a sack of bones covered with skin. He could not help but think how strong Roy had been as a young man. Once Roy was sitting in a more upright position he began to sing:

Amazing Grace, how sweet the sound,
That saved a wretch like me;
I once was lost but now am found,
Was blind but now I see.

All voices stopped and rapt attention was given to Roy. His mellow voice and his clear diction in spite of the shallow breathing, seemed so inspiring as Roy sang about His Saviour. The nurses were absorbed in the song and amazed at their patient. When he came to sing the final verse there was hardly a dry eye in the room as Roy mustered all his strength to express his confident hope for his final song:

When we've been there ten thousand years,
Bright shining as the sun.
We've no less days to sing His praise,
Than when we first begun.

It was a memorable occasion for all. Roy was not only sure that he was going to heaven, but he was very much aware that he would soon be there. It was probably this perception that prompted Roy to ask Alec McCarroll to purchase a New Testament and bring it to him in hospital. Alec was glad to oblige, and on the following Sunday took it with him when the Quintet went again to visit Roy at the Royal Victoria Hospital.

When they arrived Joan was already there. At Roy's request, she had brought their two sons, Philip and Gary, to visit their dad.   Some time after Alec had given Roy the New Testament he had requested, Roy asked for his son Philip to sit on the bed beside his dad. Campbell Archer remembers, "The atmosphere was laden with emotion and a sense of occasion. Roy slowly unwrapped the package that contained the New Testament and turning to his young son he said, 'Philip, I want to give you some thing that is very precious. You know that your mummy is very precious to you and to me. You two boys are also very precious to your mammy and daddy. But this book is the most precious thing we have on earth. Take it with you and always remember that your daddy has given you the most precious thing in the world - God's Word.' Tears ran freely down our faces, and some of us had to leave the ward. We could not stifle our emotions any longer."

Providentially, at the time Roy was sinking, Alec was admitted for surgery at the same hospital. Consequently he was able to spend some precious moments with his friend and colleague during the closing days of Roy's life.   At 6:00 a.m.

Tommy, Roy's brother, wakened Alec and simply said, "Alec, he's gone. The big fellow's gone." Alec was stunned even though he had been expecting this news. Later he quietly stood with the family and freely wept as he remembered this great servant of God.

From the day that Roy had first consulted his doctor until the day he died was no more than fifteen weeks. Roy's death was sad and yet very triumphant. His friends knew they would never hear again Roy's mellow voice sing the quartet classic *Victory in Jesus*:

> I heard an old, old story,
> How the Saviour came from glory
> To give His life on Calvary
> To save a wretch like me
> I heard about His groaning,
> Of His precious blood atoning
> Then I repented of my sins
> And won the victory
>
> *O Victory in Jesus, my Saviour, forever*
> *He sought me and bought me*
> *With His redeeming blood*
> *He loved me ere I knew Him*
> *And all my love is due Him*
> *He plunged me to victory*
> *Beneath the cleansing flow.*

It has been said, "Nothing is lost when we know where it is." In that sense no one spoke of "losing" Roy. However, he was so tall in stature, so big in heart and so great in faith, his departure left a great void in every area his life had touched.

Sometimes one can only understand the mystery of God's will when one looks back. It is only with hindsight one seems to have "20/20 vision." Roy's death was felt most acutely by his family. A singer can always be replaced, even though it was felt it would be virtually impossible to replace Roy Melville, but how can a family replace a loving husband and a kind father? Nevertheless, Roy was also greatly missed by the Quintet. They missed his company, his humour, his counsel, his talent and his ministry.

Campbell Archer's admittance to the Quintet was not planned with any forethought of Roy Melville's illness. No one expected Roy would die within such a short time. Nevertheless, Campbell, a natural baritone, was a worthy replacement for Roy and was obviously the Lord's provision. As the Quintet took time to reflect on the development of the previous months they were amazed again to see how the Lord had been planning for them even when they were not aware of God's ways.

An interesting incident was yet to follow as a result of Roy's testimony in hospital. An invitation was extended to the Quintet to sing at the 1973 Elim Easter Convention at the Royal Albert Hall in London. It was a long standing engagement, and the men had been looking forward to it for almost a year. Anticipating that Roy would be with them, they had booked six seats for the flight to and from London. Of course, because of his weakness, Roy was not able to go. Joan had got his suit dry-cleaned for the trip to London but even when she brought it home she realised her husband was not up to the journey. Both Joan and Roy wept as did Roy's colleagues in the Quintet. Big Roy would be greatly missed on the trip.

Once the five other members of the singing group boarded the aircraft they found that they had been allocated to six seats together. Two rows of three chairs faced each other. Roy's absence was poignantly brought home to them when they took their places and then looked on the empty sixth seat. No one wanted to mention it but the sullen glances at the vacant place and subsequent sensitive shake of the head was enough to reveal what were their inner most thoughts.

Once the airliner climbed into the sky and reached its cruising altitude the Quintet burst into song just as they would have done when they travelled in the car. They witnessed and sang all the way to London. It was an exhilarating opportunity and the Quintet took full advantage of it.

The experience of singing in the Royal Albert Hall was unforgettable. Ten thousand people attended the Convention and the Woodvale were given a part in every service. They sang from full hearts. They were all dressed uniformly in matching suits. More importantly, their songs were uplifting and inspiring and the arrangements were highly valued by all. The visit was one of great highlights of the long history of one of Ulster's longest existing and best loved Quintets.

During the trip Roy's companions missed his natural charisma, his sincerity in service, his quality of voice and his infectious sense of humour. The wit and banter in which George and Roy frequently indulged and with which they made many trips an unforgettable experience, was greatly missed during that long weekend.

On Easter Tuesday they boarded their return British European Airways flight for Belfast. To the surprise of all they found they were allocated the same seats as on the outward flight. Just as they settled into their seats a young man came down the aisle to take what had been Roy's empty seat. Unwittingly the young man was captivated and fascinated as once more the group sang the gospel all the way to Belfast.

In conversation between songs some of the boys spoke to their young fellow passenger about the purpose of the trip to

London. They told him about the place he was occupying and how their friend Roy wasn't able to make the trip but was seriously ill. The young man was greatly touched.

When they arrived at the Aldergrove Airport terminal the passengers disembarked from the aircraft in line and were soon greeted by their waiting friends and family. The Quintet's fellow passenger was met by his sister who immediately recognised the five singers and exclaimed, "I know who you are. I remember you all sang in Roy Melville's ward at the Royal Victoria Hospital. I was the staff nurse on duty and attended Roy the day he sang *Amazing Grace*. I'll never forget it."

At that her brother spoke up and said, "I'll never forget my trip from London. These fellows sang us all the way home, and I sat in the seat of the big fellow who is seriously ill."

Only eternity will disclose what was accomplished through this amazing but not co-incidental, episode. Not until then will we know the full impact of Roy's short but effective ministry in Word and song. It is sufficient to say that the same nurse and her brother became Christians, and that she also became a member of the same church as George Whitely.

Roy's death was mourned by thousands of people who attended his funeral. The small Cliftonpark Avenue Baptist Church was packed to capacity with all their overflow rooms filled. Well over a thousand people stood outside in the sunshine of that summer morning and listened to the funeral service over the relayed loudspeakers. Pastor Mullen had been invited to take part in the service but was unable to attend; Pastor Jack Bradley led the service. Pastor Victor McWilliams who had grown to be a great friend to the Quintet, and to Roy in particular, gave a worthy tribute and preached a comforting and challenging sermon. Afterwards the Carnmony cemetery was crowded with a great gathering of people who had come to pay their last respects to a man who had blessed them many times with his Christian ministry.

The remaining members of the Quintet were invited to sing at the Funeral Service but were too overcome with emotion to take any part. However, through the tears there was a sense of triumph which was fittingly echoed in the hymn Roy had frequently sung with his Quintet friends:

I heard about a mansion,
He has built for me in glory,
And I heard about the streets of gold,
Beyond the crystal sea;
About the angels singing,
And the old redemption story,
And some sweet day I'll sing up there
The song of victory.

O Victory in Jesus, my Saviour, forever;
He sought me and bought me,
With His redeeming blood,
He loved me ere I knew Him,
And all my love is due Him;
He plunged me to victory,
Beneath the cleansing flow.

CHAPTER SIX

Give The World A Smile

--- ❖ ---

TO LAUGH IS NOT A SIN, AND THE ABILITY TO LAUGH AT ONE'S SELF IS NOT ONLY A VIRTUE, IT is also a helpful safety valve in the pressures of life's work. Having the capacity to interject wholesome humour in a tense and nervous situation is a rare gift. Over the years the Woodvale members have been greatly endowed with a copious measure of healthy humour that has allowed them to laugh at their own mistakes and some embarrassing moments.

Roy Melville and George Whitely were blessed with a great sense of humour. George, who was a glazier, sometimes arrived at the church hall straight from work for the Thursday evening practice. As soon he entered the room the aroma of putty filled the air. Roy whimsically remarked "Our Chief Putty Officer has arrived!" George would sometimes remark about the fellow glazier who had fixed thirteen broken panes of glass before he realised it was his own spectacles that were cracked.

One night the Quintet were travelling in Roy's Toyota car en route to Ballymena Baptist for a special engagement. The new traffic system around the Co. Antrim town seemed to be like a Chinese maze. Roy was confused and frustrated as he negotiated his way through the labyrinth of narrow streets on the dark winter night. His bewilderment was made worse by the various directions of his back seat drivers and the fact they were already late for the meeting. Finally, he drove up another narrow street which he calculated was in the general direction of the local Baptist Church. Halfway up the street a policeman stepped out and waved the car down. Roy stopped the car and lowered the window. The officer of the law informed him that he was driving in the wrong direction up a "one way street." To this Roy politely answered, "We are only going one way, sir. It is the only way we know where we might find the Baptist Church." The constable laughed and then confirmed that the church was at the top of the "wrong end" of the one way street. He turned a blind eye and waved them on through in the more convenient but unlawful direction.

George Whitely especially had the ability to see the funny side of most situations. On one occasion when visiting Israel Denis Kennedy broke a tooth during an outing and had to have what was remaining of the root extracted at a Jerusalem dental clinic. When he arrived back home to Northern Ireland George told the friends that Denis had discovered his "Jewish extraction" while in Jerusalem.

Besides singing for the conventional meetings in churches and mission halls the Quintet also dedicated a lot of time singing at the various hospitals. On these visits they went from ward to ward meeting the patients, speaking a personal word to them and then uplifting them all with some inspirational singing.

The Quintet were given the opportunity by the Rev. Tom Hartley for them to sing on the Hospital Radio at the

Whiteabbey Hospital. In the recording studio the men all clustered around one microphone and sang out their usual brand of gospel music. While they were singing a familiar piece, Harry Yates must have been day-dreaming and absentmindedly forgot to come in on a leading line. After the momentary but embarrassing silent pause in the middle of the musical flow, Harry, instead of continuing with the song, blurted, "Sorry!" The whole group dissolved into fits of laughter live on the radio. The listeners must have thought it was a radio comedy.

The Elim Easter Convention of UK churches in 1973 was at the Royal Albert Hall in London, and it was an outstanding event. The famous Royal Albert Hall which had been used for many momentous occasions, now echoed with the praises of the Saviour as ten thousand Christians filled it to capacity and sang the great hymns of the Christian faith. For three days the Woodvale Quintet sang the gospel and led the great congregation in song after which the Word of God was powerfully preached.

In spite of all the years the Quintet had been singing, there was still an initial apprehension when they stood before such a large gathering. Such panic has the ability of paralysing one's thoughts. With this in mind the Quintet felt they should play safe and start their programme with one of their well-rehearsed and familiar songs, *He Touched Me*. In the Woodvale arrangement of this Gaither song Dennis Kennedy was the lead singer, and he sang the first verse as a solo before the others added their supporting voices at the chorus. Just as Campbell Archer played the introductory music, Dennis leaned over and anxiously whispered, "Campbell, what is the first line of the hymn?" The sensitive microphone picked up the comment and the congregation sensed the panic. Alec spoke up to relieve the embarrassing situation, "Leave it to an Irishman!" Spontaneous laughter rippled around the great hall. Once they had started singing their first song the music flowed smoothly for rest of the convention.

On Easter Monday morning they were part of the great march of witness to London's Trafalger Square where an open air meeting was convened. More than four thousand on-lookers converged around the famous Nelson's Pillar and nearby fountains as the Quintet sang out the gospel. The Word of God was preached, and sixteen people trusted Jesus Christ as Saviour on that occasion.

As on the trip to London the Quintet were often required to travel without their wives. These trips also meant taking time off from work which for some members involved a loss of wages. On one occasion they were in Newcastle on Tyne for a long weekend. George Whitely phoned home to Belfast since his wife had not been too well. "Where are you?" she asked.

"I'm in Newcastle," answered George.

There was a short silence after which Sadie ventured, "If you are in Newcastle it shouldn't be long until you are home." Sadie was confused and thought George was speaking of Newcastle, County Down which is only thirty miles down the road from their home, instead of Newcastle on Tyne in northeast England.

Travelling thousands of miles on Ulster's winding roads without an accident in all these years is a testimony to the gracious providence of God in protecting the Quintet. Added to all this travel there has always been the impending threat that terrorism has brought to Ulster for almost thirty years. Not once in all this time have the lads in the Quintet suffered in any way because of the situation.

One night while they were returning from a meeting in Stewartstown they were singing while the driver negotiated the dark roads of county Tyrone. Campbell Archer sat in the rear seat of the car playing his guitar while they all sang. The singing was possibly a distraction to the driver, and before long they realised they were lost. Spotting two young men walking along the road they stopped the car to ask for directions. As the two young fellows looked into the car and all they could see was the shadowy figure of Campbell holding the long neck of the guitar. Convinced it was a sinister weapon they didn't take time to answer the inquiry. The two lads jumped straight through the nearest hedge and took off over the fields - the Woodvale had been mistaken for a gang of fearsome terrorists!

On another occasion they went to a particular church, and for the first time they were all smartly attired in their stylish new matching suits. The Woodvale have always insisted that they dress well and felt they should be good ambassadors for the Lord as they sang. One older brother in the church was not too impressed with their new navy suits and accused them of copying worldly trends. "Remember," said the brother, "Jesus said it's by their fruits you shall know them, not by their suits."

A lot of perseverance was required to find some of the outlying places where the Quintet were asked to sing. "Ah, you'll find it," is what the church secretary often said. On one occasion the Woodvale went to four different churches in one town before they found the one in which they were booked to sing at.

Harry Oliver, apart from his association and participation in the Woodvale for many years, he also sang solo. On one occasion the nervous leader of a meeting welcomed Harry as the special "socialist" for the meeting. Harry being involved in sales for many years often took the responsibility of promoting the Woodvale's cassettes and CDs at the various meetings. One night he jestingly showed the cassette to the congregation and told them that while the cassette cost £6.00

Photographic
SECTION

The original Woodvale Quartette
Left to right: A. McCarroll, A. Taggart, H. Yates and J. Adams

The Woodvale Quintet in 1969
Left to right: A. McCarroll, W. Ennis, J. Gardiner, G. Whitley and H. Yates

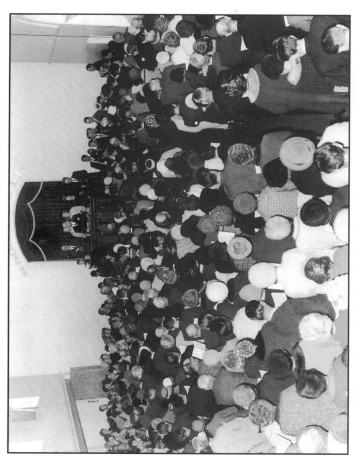

The Evangelical Mission at Lurgan Baptist Church, 1969.
Evangelist Pastor W. Mullan, Music by The Woodvale Quintet.

The Quintet singing on board a fishing vessel in Peterhead, Scotland. Superintendent of Deep Sea Mission and Pastor Victor McWilliams look on.

The Quintet venture into recording. This photo for the record's sleeve was taken a year before Roy Melville (fourth from left) died.

The Quintet in 1977. Left to right: Denis Kennedy, Alec McCarroll, Campbell Archer, John Gardiner, and George Whitley.

*The Quintet in 1978 join Rev. William McCrea for 'Evenings of Praise'
all over Ulster. Ian McDowell (organist) and Paul Gardiner (guitar).*

The Quintet in 1983. Andrew Gardiner (fourth from left) replaced Campbell Archer as baritone and guitarist.

A Singspiration Night at Harry Oliver's barn, Killinchy, Co. Down.

Harry Oliver (second left) adds his talents to the Quintet which thereafter became known as **'The Woodvale'**

The Woodvale at the Crescent Church, Belfast.
Douglas Cowan and Richard Crawford (musicians) are at the front without jackets.

Victor Maxwell pays a visit to a practice session in Cliftonpark Avenue Baptist Church.

The Woodvale at Cullybackey Elim Church with Wesley Kane, their invited preacher.

A special weekend of Testimony and Song at Ebenezer Gospel Hall, Airdrie, Scotland.

in total, the photo of the Woodvale group on the cover was worth a fiver while the actual cassette only cost £1.00. After the meeting a Scottish lady spoke to Harry and offered him a pound explaining that she really only wanted the cassette, and she wasn't interested in the accompanying photo!

In 1979 the Quintet and their wives went to Israel in the company of Rev. William McCrea, Mr. & Mrs. Fred Orr and Victor Maxwell. The ninety-six tourist who travelled together came from different parts of the world - Ulster, England, Scotland, Switzerland, the United States, New Zealand and Brazil. As they got to know each other they soon became friends and many will recall the trip as an unforgettable experience. Fred Orr's rich Bible ministry, William McCrea's inspirational singing and the daily contributions of the Quintet made the visits to the various Biblical sites an outstanding experience. Appropriately the Woodvale sang, *I Believe in a Hill Called Mount Calvary* on the very site of Golgatha; at the Garden Tomb they inspirationally gave immense expression and meaning to Bill Gaither's song *Because He Lives* as they sang:

God sent His Son, they called Him Jesus,
He came to love, heal and forgive.
He gave His life to buy my pardon,
An empty grave is there to prove my Saviour lives.

And because He lives, I can face to tomorrow
Because He lives, all fear is gone,
Because I know He holds the future,
My life is worth the living just because He lives.

Tears flowed unashamedly from many in the group as they listened to the Quintet sing with great feeling and emotion. It was one of those moments they would love to have frozen as a still frame in their minds and preserved it as a memory forever. The tour guide, Mr. Avner Ram, an unconverted Jew, was so greatly moved as the Woodvale sang *He Touched Me,* that he asked Alec to write out the words of the song for him. That same night Avner requested for the Quintet to sing the same song again.

In Jericho city we were all royally entertained by an Arab family who owned a large fruit shop. After our entourage had been served with a replenishment of fruit for the long drive to Galilee our Arab friends brought out their small tom-tom drums. With the tom-toms between their knees they began to beat a rhythm with their hands and fingers. Spontaneously the group started up a few well known Ulster songs, the like of which had never been heard in Jericho before.

Big George Whitely took the floor and much to the delight of all he pranced and carried on with the Arabs. He was an instant success with the large hand-clapping crowd of tourists and the much amused Arabs. Once he had gained their friendship George then called the boys of the Quintet together and said to the Palestinians, "Now we want to sing you a few songs from our country and about our Saviour."

In contrast to the fun and prancing about of a few minutes earlier both Arabs and the touring party listened with rapt attention as the Quintet sang the all-time quartet favourite *The Jericho Road.*

As you travel along, on the Jericho Road
Does the world seem all wrong, and heavy your load?
Just bring it to Christ, your sins all confess,
On the Jericho Road your heart He will bless.

On the Jericho road,
There's room for just two,

No more and no less,
Just Jesus and you;
Each burden He'll bear,
Each sorrow He'll share,
There's never a care
For Jesus is there.

On the Jericho Road, Bartimaeus he sat,
His life was a void, so empty and flat,
But Jesus appeared, one word brought him sight,
On the Jericho Road, Christ banished his night.

This was followed by William McCrea joining the Quintet to sing Oswald J. Smith's great hymn about Blind Bartimaues -*Then Jesus Came and Set the Captive Free.* Soon the whole group was singing out the praises of our Lord where once Jesus walked, and all this in the very place where Zachaeus, the richest man in town, and Bartimaeus, the poorest man in town, were saved by God's marvellous grace.

One sat alone beside the highway begging,
His eyes were blind, the light he could not see;
He clutched his rags and shivered in the shadows,
Then Jesus came and bade His darkness flee.

When Jesus comes the tempter's power is broken;
When Jesus comes the tears are wiped away,
He takes the gloom and fills the life with glory,
For all is changed when Jesus comes to stay.

So men today have found the Saviour able,
They could not conquer passion lust and sin;
Their broken hearts had left them sad and lonely,
Then Jesus came and dwelt, Himself within.

The week in Jerusalem was spent at the Capitalina Hotel on the Nablus Road. All of the staff there were Palestinians. In typical Ulster fashion a friendly camaraderie was struck up with the waiters and hotel kitchen staff during the week. For the first two nights some Arab and Jewish meals were served. The Ulster stock, not being known for their exotic tastes, soon made it known that they preferred plain fare. Thereafter, it was fish and chips or mashed potatoes and steaks during the rest of the stay at that hotel. Denis Kennedy even persuaded the chef to make champ, a famous Ulster dish of mashed potatoes, spring onions, milk and butter.

Little did they know, but there was a price to be paid for these culinary favours. Near the end of the week the head waiter announced in the dining room that his sister had just given birth to a baby and blood donors were needed at the clinic. Without too much thought Alec and George offered to contribute some good Ulster blood to flow in the Arab woman's veins.

The experience at the Palestinian clinic was more than they had bargained for as conditions were rather basic. Both men were shown the way to a room and instructed to lie down on rusty enamelled tables which were still stained with the blood of former donors or victims. On the floor around them lay the used and bloody swabs of other surgical procedures prior to their arrival. The tables lay parallel to each other, and Alec joked with George in an attempt to hide his apprehension for what was about to happen.

A rough torque was wrapped around their upper right arms by a male nurse while a white-coated medic swabbed their inner arms with what they hoped was disinfectant. Both Alec and George anxiously looked away in the other direction when an unlikely looking doctor dressed in casual and short Bermudas and still smoking a cigarette with a long ash on the end, produced a long needle and syringe to jab into their now protruding veins.

Finally, after a few painful attempts at penetrating their veins and another discomforting jag, they were assured the doctor that he had at last had struck blood. The torque was immediately released and blood began to pulsate into a bottle at the end of the stretcher bed. The doctor then asked with a thick Arab accent, "Can you give us two pints?" Both men immediately and excitedly protested that they would give only one pint of their vital fluid. By this time the two gullible Woodvale donors were sorry they had ever volunteered as they anxiously watched their rich Ulster blood run down the sides of an empty jar.

When the procedure was completed, the needles were removed and the puncture was covered over with a piece of cotton wool which they secured in place by their index fingers. Each of the men was asked if he preferred a drink of coffee or orange. Due the heat of the day both asked for orange. The medic unceremoniously broke the tab off a tin of local brew and handed one each to Alec and George - their reward for the donated blood.

The men survived the experience and were able to join the party again. After a few hours in bed back at the hotel they were able to join the rest of the Quintet to sing at the evening praise session. However, on return to Northern Ireland both men required some respite to recover from the Palestinian episode.

Yes, humour has a fitting place to play in the Woodvale's ministry, and it can be said to their credit that they have been able to smile at their own gaffes. They enjoy their music and through it they endeavour to communicate the joy of serving their Lord. Perhaps this joy is best expressed in one of their favourite songs, *Give the World a Smile*:

Are you giving the world a smile,
Helping lessen someone's dreary mile?
Do you greet the world with song,
As through life you pass along,
Cheering those whom you may meet
Along life's way?

Give the world a smile each day,
Helping someone on life's way,
From the paths of sin,
Bring the wanderer in,
To the Master's fold to stay,
Help to cheer lone and sad,
Help to make some pilgrim glad,
Let your life so be,
That all the world might see,
The joy of serving Jesus with a smile.

Just a bright and sunny smile will win,
Many souls from dreary paths of sin.
Lift them up to higher ground,
Where they hear the glad refrain,
Of the smiling band of workers,
On life's way.

CHAPTER SEVEN

Precious Memories

❖

MEMORY IS A WONDERFUL GIFT WHICH GOD HAS
GIVEN TO EACH ONE OF US, BUT SOMETIMES
when recalling details it can fail us. The story is told of a farmer
who lived in a remote part of Ireland. A census was being
conducted in their isolated rural area on the west coast. The
old farmer was being questioned by the census taker and was
having trouble remembering the dates of birth for his children
and grandchildren. He called out and asked his wife when one
of the girls was born. "Well," answered the wife, "I know she
was born in the potato season, but I am not sure if it was when
we were plantin' potatoes or diggin' them!"

During the five decades of the Woodvale's music ministry
there have been many monumental memories to look back on.
Some of these recollections were in times of sowing the good
seed of the Word of God, while other reminiscences were of
bringing in the harvest of precious souls - memories of a

planting season and a digging season. The Quintet have not only conducted thousands of meetings themselves but they were also greatly involved with many servants of God in some very fruitful evangelistic Missions and Bible Conferences.

Pastor Willie Mullan was a man of exceptional gift in preaching and communicating. In his remarkable testimony he told how the Lord saved him as tramp in Newtownards, and without formal theological education he developed an exceptional ministry in Ulster and abroad. His straightforward and dynamic preaching only accentuated the uniqueness of this servant of God. When Pastor Mullan began his evangelistic activities in Newtownards he was often accompanied by the Ards Trio, a group of men from the Newtownards Baptist Church where Mr. Mullan was in fellowship. Using the Ards Trio was an early indicator of how much the evangelist valued the accompanying musical ministry in his work for the Lord. In later years he also combined with Joe Nabney whom he labelled as "Ulster's gospel tenor."

High in Pastor Mullan's estimation of gospel singers was the Woodvale Quintet. In 1969 Lurgan Baptist Church decided to conduct an Evangelistic Mission in their own Church with Pastor Mullan as the evangelist. For this three week series of meetings they invited the Woodvale Quintet to minister in song every night. On the first night of the Evangelistic Mission people queued to gain admittance to the church on Windsor Avenue. Some were disappointed when there was no room for them in the building which was filled to capacity. In order to accommodate the crowds on the following nights the church immediately arranged to have closed circuit television installed in the neighbouring warehouse of Gratten's General Store where an overflow crowd filled that building and watched the service and Pastor Mullan preach on the screen. The congregational singing in both buildings was enthusiastic and inspirational as hundreds of people combined their voices in praise and worship.

The Quintet's ministry was stirring, touching and effective. They carefully selected pieces which presented the gospel message every evening and sang from full hearts. Pastor Mullan captivated his listeners with his unique style of direct and dynamic evangelistic preaching night after night. The atmosphere in every meeting was charged with a sense of God's presence. Saints rejoiced to hear the gospel message sung and preached with such clarity and power. Sinners wept in the meetings, and although no public appeal was made many got right with God before they went home. During the three weeks, scores of people professed faith in Jesus Christ - those were days of heaven on earth.

This was only one of the many occasions in which the Quintet shared in meetings with this great favourite of Ulster's gospel preachers. They accompanied him to other evangelistic endeavours at the Coalmen's Mission at the Belfast Coal Quay. No one who attended those meetings will ever forget "Wee Sammy Spence" leading the meeting and keeping the timing of the music with the thump of his foot on the platform floor. After the Quintet sang and Pastor Mullan preached, "Big Pop Stewart" asked all to bow their heads and close their eyes while he made the gospel appeal like few others could ever do. Again, dozens of people were converted at those meetings.

Pastor Mullan made a permanent place for the Woodvale Quintet each year in the missionary convention at Lurgan Baptist Church until the end of his ministry there.

As well as the very successful evangelistic enterprises with Pastor Mullan the Quintet shared in extended periods of gospel outreach with Val English at Monkstown Baptist, with George Bates and Ivan Thompson at Rathcoole Baptist and Victor Maxwell also had the privilege of sharing with them for another evangelistic mission at Monkstown Baptist Church. In all these evangelistic ventures many lives were touched and transformed by the power of God. These endeavours were only a part of the great harvest in which the Woodvale Quintet have been privileged to work.

In the late sixties there was a very close bond of fellowship and friendship between pastors Willie Mullan, Jim Irvine of Newcastle Baptist and Victor McWilliams of Kilkeel Baptist. These men held similar theological positions and often enjoyed sharing in rich Bible conference ministry in various parts of Ulster. Almost invariably, the Quintet was invited to be part of these occasions and thereby they greatly benefited from the overflow of the special relationship that existed between the three pastors.

The Woodvale co-operated with these preachers in evangelistic enterprise not only in their respective churches but also in various tent missions throughout the countryside and evangelistic excursions across the Irish Sea. Jock McCormick approached Alec McCarroll towards the end of the Donegall Road Singers' long ministry in 1973 to share with him how their group had decided to cut back on their more distant engagements. He therefore suggested that the Woodvale Quintet take their place at special meetings which had been arranged in Peterhead, a fishing village on Scotland's Northeast coast.

This development opened an annual opportunity to return to Peterhead where they had great meetings at the Deep Sea Fishermen's Mission and other local churches. On one particular visit they invited Pastor Victor McWilliams to accompany them as the guest speaker. Victor was pastor at Kilkeel Baptist where Ulster's biggest fishing fleet is based on the County Down coast. He had never travelled by airplane before and found it to be a nerve-wrecking experience made worse by the five singer's banter and agitation during the flight.

After a weekend of fruitful ministry in the Word and song, Pastor McWilliams and the Quintet were invited to join a fishing crew going to sea. If the airplane flight was harrowing for him, the boat trip he found to be even worse. These Ulster land lubbers felt they were being tossed like corks in a frenzied sea. Despite this the group sang some of the great songs about the sea such as *Master the Tempest is Raging* and *Let the Lower Lights be Burning* While the harrowed preacher and singers all survived the ordeal they were very glad to return to *terra firme*. They certainly had confirmation that their vocation was definitely not on the ocean wave.

Their continued involvement with Pastor Mullan over many years resulted in them being invited to take part in a special Memorial Service for the Lurgan pastor after his tragic death in 1981. Undoubtedly that was one of the saddest meetings in which the Quintet ever had to participate. The Memorial Service was held in the Ulster Hall in Belfast, and people came from all over the Province in memory of their beloved friend and pastor. Every seat in the hall was filled. Pastor Jack Mitchell of the Iron Hall led the proceedings, and all present listened with rapt attention as Dr. Ian Paisley spoke eloquently and powerfully of this great servant of God.

The Woodvale Quintet sang their tribute to Pastor Mullan with some of the great gospel songs they had formerly sung when they had accompanied him at evangelistic missions and Bible conferences. One of these songs was of special interest - *Wonderful Saviour*. Pastor Mullan was quite skilled at expressing great biblical truths in verse and some of his poems were published both as prose and in song. Some years prior to the death of Willie Mullan, the Woodvale boys were invited to a weekend engagement at the famous Curruber's Close in Edinburgh. Dr. John Moore, author of the great favourite,

Burden's are Lifted at Calvary and many other hymns, told the Woodvale singers that he had received a few verses of prose from Willie Mullan. He explained that he had always planned to put the verses to music but had never got round to doing so. He decided to take advantage of the Woodvale being with him that weekend and composed the music to match the text. The music was ideally suited to the five-voice harmony, and during that weekend in Edinburgh the Quintet sang Pastor Mullan's hymn, *Wonderful Jesus,* for the first time .

Wonderful Jesus

Wonderful Jesus, Saviour of men,
Wonderful Jesus, right to the end,
Wonderful Jesus, setting me free,
Wonderful Jesus, eternally.

Wonderful Jesus, drying my tears,
Wonderful Jesus, calming my fears,
Wonderful Jesus, pleading for me,
Wonderful Jesus, eternally.

Wonderful Jesus, preparing a place,
Wonderful Jesus, sufficient my grace,
Wonderful Jesus, there on the tree,
Wonderful Jesus, eternally.

Wonderful Jesus, coming someday,
Wonderful Jesus, forever I'll say,
Wonderful Jesus, my song shall be,
Wonderful Jesus, eternally.

It is interesting to note that it was at the same Curruber's Close Mission one hundred years earlier that the famous American Evangelist, Dwight L. Moody, conducted an evangelistic mission and at one of the meetings Moody's noted soloist, Mr. Ira Sanky, sang for the first time the greatly renowned hymn *The Ninety and Nine*. It is reputed that Mr. Moody had preached a powerful sermon from Luke chapter fifteen in which he majored on the parables of the Lost Sheep, the Lost Coin and the Lost Son. When he had finished preaching he invited Mr. Sankey to sing a solo. Earlier that day Ira Sankey had read a poem published in a local paper where a mother had written about her prodigal son as being, "out on the mountains wild and bare and far from the tender Shepherd's care." Sanky sat at the organ in Curruber's Close Mission and composed the music to fit the poem even as he sang. The famous hymn was born and the music remains unchanged to this very day. Pastor Mullan's composition was in very good company.

Several months after that visit to Dr. Moore in Edinburgh the Woodvale took their place at the annual missionary convention at Lurgan Baptist. On the Saturday night in front of a packed church before a packed church they stood to announce a new piece they had recently learned. To Pastor Mullan's great surprise the five boys sang the lyrics of his newly composed hymn. He was totally taken aback and as soon as they had finished he asked them to sing it again. It was a great occasion, and Pastor Mullan was greatly touched that the Quintet had sung the hymn for the him in his own church. Now they were invited to sang the same hymn at his memorial service. It was a very moving occasion.

In the spring of 1977 at Belfast's Wellington Hall one Saturday afternoon, the Woodvale boys were rehearsing with

Rev. William McCrea. They were singing a favourite of the time, *Learning to Lean on Jesus*. That night was the first of numerous gospel concerts they would share with William McCrea that would take them all the way from Belfast's Ulster Hall to many civic centres and town halls throughout Northern Ireland and to the famous Mansion House in Dublin, the Guild Hall in Londonderry, across the Irish Sea to other venues and then in more recent times to the modern and majestic Waterfront Concert Hall in Belfast. Thousands of people attended those meetings, and as a result, scores of people were converted.

That first gathering in the Wellington Hall was an innovative venture as "Evenings of Praise" and gospel concerts were a relatively new approach at that time. The Christian public responded enthusiastically and turned up in their thousands. Nearly two hours before opening the doors long queues formed down Wellington Place in Belfast city centre. The crowds were so great that not only were the YMCA's main hall and the minor hall filled to more than capacity but hundreds of people had to be turned away.

A few months later when a similar gathering was repeated the overflow crowd, so eager to see the concert, gatecrashed the main Wellington Hall to gain entrance. The stewards were helpless in their efforts to control the surge of people. Hundreds stood at the rear of the large hall blocking the vital fire escape routes. As a result of this overcrowding those responsible for convening these gospel concerts were banned from using the Wellington Hall again. Sadly, within a year the famous old hall was closed and never replaced.

George Whitely can remember a night at Limavady Town Hall where they sang the gospel for almost three hours to a full house with the Rev. William McCrea. George recalls, "At the end of the evening nine people trusted the Saviour. One of those was an eighty-five year old man who said that although he had always been a religious man he had never heard the gospel in such a simple way before and he wanted to be saved. I had the joy of leading him in the simple steps of repentance from sin and into faith in Jesus Christ."

For Campbell Archer the best night he can recall as part of the Quintet was at the Newtownards Town Hall when again the public building was packed beyond its capacity. A full and extravagant programme of supporting singers complimented the Woodvale and William McCrea in a great night of witness and praise. At the end of that service five people trusted the Lord Jesus as Saviour. Today three of those converts are members of the Cornerstone Community Church in Newtownards of which Campbell Archer has been pastor for eight years.

Besides the live gospel concerts and Evenings of Praise that were conducted all over the Province, the Woodvale have also been able to make many audio and visual recordings over a period of thirty years. The first recording contract happened quite inadvertently. Norman Bisset, whom Alec had known at the shipyard in his unconverted days, had been converted and was actively engaged in singing the gospel around Belfast. He arranged to cut a long play record with Solomon & Peres of Anne Street, which was Belfast's leading recording company at the time. One Saturday night at the Help Heavenward Meeting in the Victoria Hall, Norman approached Alec to invite the Quintet to provide him with backing voices for his recordings.

The arrangements were duly made and the group went to the studios and provided the backing voices for each of Norman's fourteen pieces. The producer, Mr. Jim Gunner, was really impressed with the quality of the Quintet sound and asked them to consider recording their own LP record with Solomon

& Peres. Mr. Mervyn Solomon himself, a director of the recording company, liked their sound and with *Amazing Grace* topping the secular charts in the USA and United Kingdom, he felt the Woodvale had good enough harmony and music to sing favourite gospel songs.

At the Emerald Studios the five fellows were accompanied by various musicians who in later years would make a name for themselves in other fields; George Jones, now a favourite presenter every afternoon on Radio Ulster, was on bass guitar; Jim Gunner played lead guitar; Tommy Thomas was at the drums; and Ivan Black, also of Radio Ulster, was at the piano. The Quintet sang out the gospel, and after two sessions the recording was complete.

This was not only the first venture into the vinyl recording field for the Quintet, but they were also the first Christian group in Northern Ireland to spearhead this venture into the recording field. It soon opened the way for other Christian singers to follow.

The sale of the record was far beyond everyones expectations with more than twenty-two thousand records sold throughout Northern Ireland and Scotland, where their ministry had become increasingly popular. This quick success prompted Mr. Solomon to invite the Quintet back to his studios to record a second LP with the notable Belfast organist, Mr. Maurice McKenzie. Again this recording was very successful with over twenty thousand sold.

The ongoing development in electronic technology meant that records soon gave way to tape cassette recordings which in turn were superseded by Compact Discs and complimented by video recordings. The Quintet continued to use all these approaches and had great success with different production companies.

While many of these memories were very happy ones of great times and great people, memory however is not confined just to remembering the good days. Some of the finest contributors to the history of the Woodvale's musical ministry over the years are now with the Lord: John Adams, a founder member of the Woodvale, passed away very suddenly at the end of May 1998; Roy Melville died after his final struggle with cancer; John Gardiner was another key member in this ministry for more than thirty-five years until his home call in June 1993.

John's qualities of faithfulness and loyalty were only a few facets of his spiritual life, but physically he was not a healthy man, for he suffered from epilepsy. Notwithstanding this handicap, he seldom missed a practice in Belfast, even when he moved to live in Craigavon. While others enjoyed the benefit of their personal transport John at times was not able to take his place behind the steering wheel either because of his illness or the family car was not available. Nevertheless, for more than twenty years John commuted every Thursday, mostly on public transport, between Belfast and Craigavon for their practice session.

John was not only a great musician and enjoyed his music but he loved the Lord and His service. Although he was not a leader he was never content to sit back and do nothing. As a preacher he handled the Word of God well. John's best quality was perhaps his diligent work in bringing others to the Lord Jesus Christ. When the Quintet shared with Victor Maxwell in an evangelistic mission at Monkstown Baptist, John frequently brought his neighbours from forty miles away in Craigavon to attend those gospel meetings.

One of the nights he brought a friend who was an addicted alcoholic. With tears streaming down his face the man sought the Lord after the meeting. John Gardiner stayed with him and with the preacher pointed the alcoholic to personal faith in Jesus Christ. John then took the new convert under his wing to help nurture him in his new found faith in Jesus Christ.

On one very wet night John was driving through Lurgan for an engagement, and he saw a lonely character standing with a guitar case at the bus stop while the rain seemed to be bouncing off the ground around him. Remembering his own personal experience of suffering similar lonely and long waits in bus shelters, John pulled his car over and offered the drenched stranger a ride.

They tossed the guitar case into the rear of the car and took off in the direction the passenger needed to go, even though it was not the same course as John had originally planned. John opened up the conversation and guided towards speaking about the guitar and music. The stranger was a semi-professional musician on his way to a night club where he employed his talents. John told him of his own interest and involvement in music and proceeded to give his testimony of his conversion to Jesus Christ and his service for the Lord. The fellow promised to go and hear the Quintet sing.

After John's funeral service a gentleman approached Alec McCarroll on the street outside Portadown Elim Church and introduced himself as the stranger to whom John had given the ride in the car. He went on to tell how as a result of that conversation and the subsequent visit to hear John with the Quintet he was convicted and convinced of the emptiness and futility of his life. Because of John's practical kindness and testimony this man was converted by the grace of God. Today that stranger, Junior Mercer, is the leader of the Amen Gospel Praise Band, a group of former professional musicians who now employ their skills and talents to sing and testify to the grace of the gospel all across the country.

On 30 May, 1992, John sang with his friends in the Quintet for the last time at a meeting in the Finaghy Evangelical Church. He had been suffering from influenza prior to the meeting and although he had recovered he was still a bit off colour. John planned to return to work the following week so he went to the meeting to cover for George Whitely who had gone on holidays. The following Sunday evening, 6 June 1993, the Quintet had no engagement as it was the first Sunday of the month. John retired to bed that evening and when his wife went upstairs to join him she discovered John had gone to be with his Lord. He had died of a heart attack.

John's sudden death was a very severe blow to his family and stunned both his colleagues in Woodvale and Northern Ireland's Christian public. His funeral at Portadown Elim Church was marked by a sense of triumph and thanksgiving as close on a thousand people gathered to pay respects to their Christian brother who was greatly beloved by all and greatly used by God.

Precious memories greatly enhance the fabric of life, and John Gardiner had woven a lot into the lives of others during his years of ministry with the Woodvale Quintet.

Precious memories unseen angels,
Sent from somewhere to my soul;
How they linger, ever near me,
And the sacred past unfold.

Precious memories, how they linger,
How they ever flood my soul;
In the stillness of the midnight,
Precious, sacred scenes untold.

In the stillness of the midnight,
Echoes from the past I hear;
Old time singing, gladness bringing,
From that lovely land somewhere.

As I travel on life's pathway,
Know not what the years may hold;
As I ponder, hope grows fonder,
Precious memories flood my soul.

CHAPTER EIGHT

Because He Lives

❖

SERVICE FOR JESUS CHRIST IS A GREAT
PRIVILEGE, BUT IT IS NOT EASY AND OFTEN IT
makes great demands on the servant's time and life. Howard
Hendrick's has said, "If our service for God is going to count
then be sure it is going to cost." It was with some sacrificial
cost that Campbell Archer stepped out of his lucrative business
to study at Belfast Bible College. For some time he and
Margaret had felt the challenge of dedicating their lives fully
to the Lord's service. Besides stepping out of his secular
employment, the increased responsibilities of study at college
compelled Campbell to tender his resignation from the Quintet.
His departure was greatly lamented by the other members of
the Quintet, but they also recognised they could not resist God's
call on their colleague's life, nor would they stand in his way.

As on other occasions the remaining members of the
Quintet were faced with the dilemma of finding a suitable

replacement for this vital member of the group. For eight years Campbell had played the guitar accompaniment, as well as singing baritone. During these years he and Margaret were fully committed to the ministry of the Woodvale.

Andrew Gardiner, John's younger brother and a member of Cliftonpark Avenue Baptist Church, had always shown interest in the ministry of the Woodvale Quintet and at onetime he had been considered as a possible member. However, because of his employment, Andrew had moved to far off Enniskillen. Providentially, just when Campbell moved out into his new vocation, Andrew's job brought him and his family to live in Newtownabbey.

Like his brother John, Andrew had also been reared in a Christian home where he was taught that a true Christian should be zealous for His Lord. While living in Enniskillen, Andrew and Pauline Gardiner devoted much of their free time to the work of the gospel in County Fermanagh. This involvement in Christian work enabled Andrew to develop his preaching skills as well as put his vocal and musical ability to good use. That same enthusiastic zeal for the Lord's work continued when Andrew and Pauline transferred to Monkstown Baptist Church.

After their move, Andrew and his family were stunned when Andrew suffered a mild heart attack. Thankfully he made a good recovery after treatment at the nearby Whiteabbey Hospital. When Andrew was approached to consider replacing Campbell Archer in the Woodvale Quintet he had just been released from hospital. At first he thought the invitation was only an incentive to encourage him back to his health and strength. Besides the health scare his responsibilities with an international company in which he had been promoted were also increasing. However, when it was made clear to him that the invitation was genuine Andrew had no hesitation in joining the Quintet. He felt it was the door the Lord was opening for him.

Andrew slotted in very smoothly, and with his own style of singing and playing guitar he made his valuable contribution to the Woodvale's ministry. Right from the beginning Andrew put his competence on the guitar, his singing voice and his preaching ability to good use. For the next thirteen years the younger of the Gardiner brothers provided backing on the lead guitar, sang lead baritone with the Quintet and skilfully preached the Word of God all over Northern Ireland and beyond. The Woodvale was a big part of Andrew's life and ministry.

The regular round of meetings continued to take the Quintet to small mission halls and large church gatherings all over the United Kingdom. The Woodvale Quintet underwent another change in their development several years after Andrew joined them.

Harry Oliver was the managing director of the famous W. A Ross & Sons Mineral Water Company in Belfast. He was raised in a Christian home and his father, Mr. Anthony Oliver, was a well known elder in Newtownards Baptist Church. As a Christian business man Harry took time to develop his own ministry for the Lord. He was extremely gifted at the piano with a soft and easy touch on the keyboard which produced a very pleasant sound. In the fraternity of Ulster's Christian musicians Alec knew about the quality of Harry's talent.

George Whitely had moved to live in South Belfast and had transferred his membership from Cliftonpark Avenue to Milltown Baptist Church which was near to his new home. During the troubled years of the seventies and eighties it was unsafe to conduct the Woodvale practices at Cliftonpark Avenue so they used the facilities at Milltown Baptist Church which were kindly granted to them. In recompense for the church's kindness the Woodvale occasionally took part with other singers in an annual Evening of Praise at the Milltown Church. At one of these gatherings Harry Oliver was a guest soloist. Again the

Woodvale fellows enjoyed Harry's relaxed yet confident style and his rich baritone voice. In conversation over a cup of tea following the meeting it became evident that the Woodvale should make an approach to Harry and invite him to be part of their ministry

A few days later Alec visited Ross's office in Ravenhill Avenue and again Harry confided to Alec that while he enjoyed his ministry he envied the evident fellowship and camaraderie that existed in the Quintet. Alec asked if he would be interested in combining his talents to sing with the group. At first he thought Alec was teasing.

Harry attended the next Thursday evening practice with the group and sang some of his own arrangements. The other members of the Quintet added their range of voices in the refrain. The blend was immediate and the fellows had no hesitation to pool their talents and include Harry with the group. Thereafter the Woodvale Quintet abbreviated their name to be simply known as "The Woodvale."

There were many notable and outstanding occasions, and none greater than the night th Quintet sang at Cambridge Rooms in Park Avenue Hotel. Six-hundred people were packed into the extended room, and after a delicious meal the audience enjoyed the varied singing programme. All who attended will never forget when the Quintet joined William McCrea to sing *Where No One Stands Alone* - it was an occasion that could only be experienced rather than described or defined. Everyone felt his heart uplifted and was greatly blessed through the musical message.

While they were on the rostrum singing Alec spied Mr. Herbie Martin sitting with his wife in the vast audience. Mr. Martin had been the missioner at the Woodvale Mission in Disreali Street where the group made their tentative beginning back in 1948. He was also the man who led young Alec

McCarroll and Harry Yates to personal faith in Jesus Christ. After the Quintet finished their song Alec announced the presence of his spiritual father and asked Mr. Martin to stand up in recognition of the contribution he had made to the original Quartet. Mr. Martin, a humble man, was so pleased to identify with Alec that night. Two weeks later Herbie Martin suddenly passed into the presence of His Lord. All in the Quintet felt they had given Mr. Martin a lovely and worthy farewell before he was promoted to glory.

John Gardiner had played a vital role in the Woodvale story for over three decades and although his death was a big blow to all members of the Quintet, understandably it was Andrew who felt it most acutely. Because of the family bereavement, a few engagements were cancelled but it was felt the ministry should continue. A long standing commitment had been pledged by the Woodvale to sing each night at an evangelistic mission organised at Rathcoole Baptist Church in September 1993. The fellows duly prepared for this engagement but Andrew felt his time with the Woodvale had come to a close and he withdrew. During his thirteen years as lead guitarist and lead baritone Andrew had contributed greatly to the ministry of the Woodvale even though there were increasing demands on his time because of growing responsibilities in his secular employment. Thankfully his earlier heart complaint never returned to create any problem.

After the loss of Andrew Gardiner the Woodvale continued without a replacement lead baritone for almost one year. Harry Oliver's rich, smooth and seemingly effortless singing removed the urgency of needing to fill the vacancy immediately. One day however, a friend of Alec McCarroll at Larne Technical College drew his attention to the singing talent of her brother-in-law, Ian Mawhinney. She strongly recommended him to the musical ministry of the Woodvale.

Ian, a construction engineer, was reared in a Christian home and was a member of First Antrim Presbyterian Church. Besides using his baritone voice in the church choir he also engaged in singing solo at various church venues. Alec was a little apprehensive in approaching Ian about singing with the Woodvale in view of him and his wife Ruth having a young family, and Ian also carried a heavy responsibility in the family business. Notwithstanding these reservations, when the offer was made to consider singing with the Woodvale Ian showed immediate interest and promised to give it due thought and prayer.

After duly considering his domestic and business responsibilities Ian, fully supported by Ruth, his wife, felt this was the Lord's direction for him. Right from his first practice Ian was at home with the group. He enjoyed the rich fellowship, the high standard and quality of sound expected as well as the varied opportunities for ministry in song throughout the year.

In 1995 the Woodvale were invited to assist in a gospel mission at Comber Baptist Church when Mr. Bertie Johnson was the evangelist. As the singers took part each night they were skilfully accompanied on an acoustic guitar by the Pastor's son, Richard Crawford. At the end of the three week Mission the boys in the group were so impressed by Richard's contribution that they invited him to be part of their ministry.

Richard, a car salesman, was born into a Christian home. His parents Wesley and Helen Crawford, were missionaries for some years in Eastern Europe with the Slavic Gospel Association prior to entering pastoral ministry. Through the influence of his mum and dad, Richard was converted to the Lord Jesus when he was six years old. During school years he lost his sense of assurance of salvation and consequently drifted away from what he had first learned as a Christian. When his dad accepted an invitation to pastor Portstewart Baptist Church,

Richard came into contact with Child Evangelism Fellowship, and as a result he was restored to the reality of his Christian life.

It was through Child Evangelism Fellowship in Portstewart that Richard had his first involvement in Christian work, and this experience greatly helped his spiritual development. At the Good News Clubs and at church, Richard used his ability with the guitar to accompany and encourage the singing. He dedicated this acquired musical talent to the Lord without knowing that the Lord was preparing him when one day the door would open for him to play music all over the British Isles with the Woodvale.

With the addition of Richard Crawford to the Woodvale the five male singing voices were now supported by a leading acoustic guitar and Harry Oliver's expertise at the piano.

Each year Harry brought the Woodvale to a barn at his home where he organised an evangelistic bar-b-que. To this he invited many friends and neighbours. Besides the Woodvale, other guest singers and musicians sang and played their instruments. One of these noted musicians was Dougie Cowan who had been using his talents at these gatherings for several years. Dougie plays seven musical instruments which include, uccalili, banjo and guitar. The Woodvale boys were so impressed with the versatility of Dougie that they felt constrained to invite him to use his admirable gifts in their musical ministry.

Dougie Cowan matches, if not surpasses, George Whitely for his wit and humour. Having had the blessing of being reared in a Christian home on Belfast's Malone Road, he was converted to Jesus Christ as a child just after World War II. For many of these years he was in fellowship at Apsley Street Gospel Hall on the south side of Belfast before moving to Bangor where he now attends Holborn Gospel Hall.

With Dougie's versatility and competence on various musical instruments, he had been involved with many Christian musicians over the years. When the invitation was given to join the Woodvale he had no hesitation in giving a positive response. He plays bass guitar, and occasionally uses some of the other instruments in his contribution to compliment the present day Woodvale sound.

In May 1998 Dougie's ninety-two year old mother was in attendance at Calvary Baptist Church in East Belfast to listen to him relate the story of his conversion to Christ and then listen to the various singing contributions by the Woodvale. His testimony is evidence not only of the value of the continuing ministry of the Woodvale, but of the efficiency of the gospel of Jesus Christ who ever lives to save sinners like Dougie Cowan.

God sent His Son, they called Him Jesus,
He came to love, heal and forgive.
He bled and died to seal my pardon;
An empty grave is there to prove my Saviour lives.

Because He lives I can face tomorrow;
Because He lives all fear is gone;
Because I know He holds the future,
My life is worth the living just because He lives.

And then one day I'll cross the river,
And fight life's final war with pain,
And then when death gives way to victory,
I'll see the lights of glory and I'll know He lives.

CHAPTER NINE

This is My Story, This is My Song

❖

BEHIND EVERY HYMN THERE IS A CIRCUMSTANCE AND A STORY. WITH EVERY SINGER THERE IS A reason for singing his favourite song. The Woodvale have accumulated a great variety songs over the years. In the early years the Quintet carried a few song books alongside their Bibles or a few sheets neatly folded into their Bible. For today's engagements they carry a double size teacher's carrier bag in which hundreds of hymns are stored. Every hymn is surrounded with memories of places they have been and milestones in those memories.

Harry Oliver has been with the Woodvale singers for fifteen years. Singing has given him immense satisfaction and great joy in serving his Lord. Singing with the Woodvale has been an added privilege in that ministry. Harry comments "With the Woodvale there is a special blend and harmony amongst the lads and the fellowship we enjoy is hard to define other than to say it is unique. The fellows whole heartedly believe in what they are singing and this adds great expression to the message. They are dedicated and resolute in producing their best sound. This involves a lot of practice and committing pieces and arrangements to memory. I sit at the piano and although we don't have written music of the arrangement and adaptation of the song, yet the blend and sound is excellent and makes my contribution at the keyboard a lot easier."

Harry finds it hard to single out one hymn as a favourite, but there is a song that came to him with great impact. He recalls, "One day a young man who had been recommended for a job came to be interviewed. In the course of the conversation that ensued the young man told me his story. Like too many other young men he had got involved in terrorist organisations and as a result was sentenced to a lengthy spell behind bars. During those days of incarceration the young fellow not only had time to reflect on his life but also came into contact with other's from a similar background whose lives had been dramatically changed by their conversion to Jesus Christ. The interviewee told how his remorse for his ill advised and evil deeds turned to repentance and he also was spiritually born again. He told that his life was subsequently filled with light and now that he was released from prison he wanted to prove to his friends and family that his life was completely transformed."

Harry was moved by the young man's testimony. Just that very week he heard a piece that mirrored the experience of that former terrorist. He felt compelled to rehearse the song and sing it the following weekend.

Mercy Re-wrote My Life

For years I travelled a road all alone,
My heart had lost all its joy and its song,

Then grace placed me right where I belong,
When mercy re-wrote my life.

Mercy re-wrote my life,
Mercy re-wrote my life,
I could have fallen, my soul cast way down,
But mercy re-wrote my life.

That day my mistakes were turned to miracles,
He washed my tears and turned them all into joy,
My past sins were forgiven, a new name is written,
When mercy re-wrote my life.

The song became an instant favourite with Harry and his colleagues and well declares what God does in the lives of forgiven sinners.

Denis Kennedy indicates, "Singing is my life. While others may employ their ability to preach and speak publicly for their Lord, my ministry is two fold. I look after the buses and bussing programme at the Ulster Temple and sing the gospel of my Saviour with the Quintet. I am not a public speaker but singing with the Woodvale for thirty years has given me great satisfaction in serving the Lord Jesus.

"As a group we are our own worst critics. We all expect and aim for a very high standard. The gospel is greatest message in the world and we dare not give other than our best in singing the same message to the world. We are all individuals but the fun and fellowship is rich and has provided Moira and me with the greatest moments of our lives.

In the hundred's of hymns that we have learned and sang over the years my favourite is one we seldom sing now. *The Highest Hill* was one of Roy Mellvile's favourites, and I always enjoyed him singing the lead part. After Roy died I tried to take the lead in the hymn, and every time I sang it I could hear Roy's voice. While the memory of our friend helped me put meaning into what I was singing I found it also was too painful for me to sing."

The Highest Hill

When we climb the Highest Hill some morning,
When we've left the valley far behind,
When we've passed the road's last bend
We'll be welcomed by the Friend
Who's been watching o'er us
As we leave the trail we climb

Then that day we'll see our blessed Saviour
And we'll rest where all is calm and still.
Then He'll wipe away each tear
Every pain and every fear
When we stand upon the Highest Hill.

Then we'll sing redemption songs together
Till with joy our happy hearts shall thrill
Every care shall pass away
And we'll find a brighter day
When we stand upon the Highest Hill.

Alec McCarroll has seen all the various singers come and go and after fifty years he still goes on with the same enthusiasm and zest for singing even though his sandy hair has now turned grey. He has been greatly blessed by the support of his family in the work. As secretary for the Quintet since its inception he has records of their engagements going back decades. Alec has personally known several generations of great gospel preachers in Ulster. On the platform he is their spokesman to introduce the singers and their songs. His one remaining ambition is summed up in the words of His favourite piece,

We Shall See Jesus

Once on a hillside, people were gathered,
Watching as Jesus was crucified,
No one showed mercy, to the One Who had healed them,
Yet Jesus loved them, as He suffered and died.

We shall see Jesus, Just as they saw Him,
There is no greater promise than this,
When He returns in power and glory,
We shall see Jesus, just as He is.

Once on a hillside, people were gathered,
For Jesus had risen and soon would ascend,
But then as He blessed them, He rose to the heavens,
And He gave them this promise, To come back again.

With the abundance of modern gospel songs, many with a distinct Country and Western flavour imported from USA, it is not surprising that George Whitely still claims his favourite hymn is George Matheson's *O Love That Wilt Not Let Me Go*.

George explains, "There is no greater theme to our songs than the love of God. We never can exhaust its scope and never tire of singing it's message. My Christian life and experience has been greatly enriched by the privilege of singing with the Woodvale for over thirty-five years. I have had so many unforgettable experience's travelling with the boys all over Ulster, Ireland, Scotland and England, and I will never forget our trip to Israel. Saints have been blessed and sinners have been saved, and we have had great joy in it all. I love the hymn

O Love That Wilt Not Let Me Go because of the experience of young George Matheson who was disappointed in being refused by his fiancee when he suffered sudden blindness. His bitter experience in being let down by human love opened to him a deeper appreciation of the love of God which he describes in such a comprehensive way."

O Love That Wilt Not Let Me Go

O Love, that wilt not let me go,
I rest my weary soul in Thee;
I give Thee back the life I owe,
That in thine ocean depths, its flow
May richer, fuller be.

O Light, that followest all my way,
I yield my flickering torch to Thee;
My heart restores its borrowed ray,
That in Thy sunshine's blaze, its day
May brighter, fuller be.

O Joy, that seekest me through pain,
I cannot close my heart to Thee;
I trace the rainbow through the rain,
And feel the promise is not vain,
That morn shall tearless be.

O Cross, that liftest up my head,
I dare not ask to fly from Thee;
I lay in dust life's glory dead,
And from the ground, there blossomed red,
Life that shall endless be.

Ian and Ruth Mawhinney's Christian life was given a severe jolt back in 1990. Their five-week old baby, Stuart, manifested some malfunction in his digestive system. The surgeon told them that investigations needed to be done on the infant. There was some uncertainty about little Stuart's condition, and the parents were informed that it was either a congenital condition that had a very grave prognosis or it was another inborn malady that would need to be treated by controlled diet throughout the boy's life.

The uncertainty and gravity of the situation cast Ian and Ruth to rock bottom of their human resources. They felt they were inadequate to cope with the circumstance, and in their distress they surrendered their lives and family totally to the Lord. Providentially the baby's condition was diagnosed as the latter of these two conditions, and he survived the episode even though today he is still on the prescribed diet.

Ian admits, "When we sing the song *Every Need Supplied* I feel that is what Ruth and I proved when we passed through that painful experience with Stuart. The Lord is faithful. He answered our prayers, and He has met our every need and we found He was the solution to all our problems.

Singing with the Woodvale is an added blessing to my Christian life. I enjoy the fellowship, the good humour and above all the privilege of serving the Lord in song. I am greatly blessed when I see others being blessed in the meetings. Sometimes you see some one with tears in their eyes as we sing a piece that is obviously meaningful to that person. On occasions people seek us out to express their appreciation for the song and what it meant to them. That is the greatest satisfaction for me and makes singing with the Woodvale all worthwhile."

Every Need supplied.

I ask the dear Saviour, What He had purchased,
For me when at Calvary He died,
For all my past and all my problems,
He just said that He would provide.

Every need supplied,
Every need supplied,
Healing , cleansing, sweet peace inside,
Every need supplied,
He's all I need, He's all I need,
Jesus is all I need,
He satisfies, my need supplies,
Jesus is all I need.
Every need supplied.

If I had to name the greatest blessing,
He's given how would I decide,
After He saved me,
I just have to say,
Every need is supplied.

Richard Crawford is the youngest member of the present
Woodvale group and clearly enjoys his participation with his
colleagues in serving the Lord by singing the gospel week after
week. Richard comments, "Having been raised in a Christian
home and my dad being a pastor, I find the ministry of the
Woodvale such a blessing to my own life. The fellowship
amongst the lads is tremendous. Besides the fellowship there
is great friendship and a lot of fun as we meet the Lord's people
all over Ulster. It is hard to highlight any one meeting as being

better than the other for I enjoy them all, but perhaps a highlight for me were the nights we sang to a full house at the Waterfront Concert Hall in Belfast. The two nights with William McCrea and his friends from Ulster and singers from USA were exhilarating. Six months later we were back at the Waterfront again to sing at a very touching Memorial Service for Richard Morrow. Richard, who died after a long and gallant battle with cancer, had been a regular contributor at many evening's of praise with the Woodvale."When I was a child at school in Armagh, Richard often visited our home and he often played guitar and sang in our church. My family knew him well and I learned a lot from him about skill and technique with the guitar. It was a privilege to take part in the fitting Memorial Service to a full Waterfront Hall. Among the many hymns the Woodvale sing I have several favourites. One of these is *Beulah Land*. Songs about heaven mean a lot to me. Ten years ago my sister Deborah went to be with the Lord. She was only twenty-one years old. That makes heaven all the more precious to me and my family."

Beulah Land

I'm kind of homesick for a country,
To which I've never been before.
No sad goodbyes will there be spoken,
For time won't matter any more.

Beulah Land, I'm longing for you,
And some day on thee I'll stand;
Where my home shall be eternal;
Beulah Land, sweet Beulah Land.

I'm looking now across the river,
Where my faith will end in sight;
There's just a few more days to labour,
Then I will take my heavenly flight.

For Dougie Cowan travelling with and playing bass guitar for the Woodvale is a relatively new experience. He has been working with different groups for many years. Dougie acknowledged, "I wasn't very long with the boys when I discovered that their prime objective is to the serve the Lord in Word and in song, and there is great enthusiasm in doing so. At the rehearsals the fellowship is outstanding and the chit-chat and banter is fun. However, when it comes to practicing songs the fellows are all dedicated to do their best. We are mindful that we serve the Lord Christ. Our work is bathed in prayer, and for us it is a joy to see people blessed in the meetings.

"The actual meetings are only the tip of the iceberg in the work of the Woodvale. Planning itineraries and pieces, learning and rehearsing new pieces, study and prayer for meetings, travelling by land, sea and air and then actually ministering in the meetings call for a lot of commitment. The lads are the measure of that commitment that is called for and the Lord has been gracious to us."

"My favourite song expresses our experience as we go to serve the Lord in all different venues."

Always There For Me

Always there for me, when I'm lonely,
He's my only true Friend ,
When I'm filled with fear.
I can feel Him near,
Always there for me, My dear Lord.

Always there for me, very carefully,
Watching over me night and day,
Always there for me, meeting all my needs,
I'm so glad Jesus is always there for me.

Always there for me, when in pain,
Reassuring me that my prayers are not in vain,
Oh, and when the way is dark
And I cannot see
Faith assures me that He's always there for me.

CHAPTER TEN

Until Then

—————————————— ❖ ——————————————

IT HAS BEEN MY PLEASURE TO HAVE KNOWN
THE WOODVALE BOYS FOR MANY YEARS. I HAVE
shared both platform and pulpit with them in evangelistic
meetings and Evenings of Praise in many and places and we
recall many precious times when saints were blessed and
sinners were converted to Jesus Christ by the grace of God .

It was 6.30 p.m. on a bright spring evening when I dropped
into Cliftonpark Avenue Baptist Church as a spectator at the
weekly practice session of the Woodvale boys. The atmosphere
was informal and relaxed. The seven fellows, casually dressed
but in good voice, gathered round the piano and sang into their
hand held microphones.

My presence did not go unnoticed and soon I was invited
to commit the evening rehearsal to the Lord in prayer with
special request for the Saturday evening engagement in
Stewartstown.

Harry with opened collar and loosened tie sat at the piano keyboard as he played the introduction to *Nearer My God to Thee*. All the voices blended to sing their first hymn which ironically was the "Titanic's" sinking hymn. He had just arrived from a business engagement in Londonderry seventy miles away. Alec stood singing at one end of the piano, a mike in one hand and signalling the timing by rhythmically waving his other hand. Dougie and Richard stood behind Harry playing lead and bass guitars. Denis and Ian sat on a small table in front of the piano singing into a covered mike that like a large lollipop. George Whitely stood nearby also singing into another sponge covered microphone. Several music stands held sheets of paper with the words of each song written in extra large letters.

The five voices blended as they came to the final crescendo of their first piece. Dougie Cowan, ever the comic, reminded his friends that today was his thirty third wedding anniversary and at great sacrifice, not to mention the danger he was in, he had come to the practice without his wife. In honour of the occasion he asked them to rehearse the hymn he had requested the Woodvale to sing at his funeral as he will not be there to hear them on that day: *It Is Well With My Soul*. The other fellows teased Dougie about who would be gone to heaven first. Some one suggested that if it was Alec they would all have to be sure to be on key and pitch else there would be a knock from inside the coffin and a resurrected Alec reminding to hold key.

Soon they embarked on singing Dougie's requested hymn. Harry not only played the piano but took the leading voice and sang the first verse as a solo. The other voices joined in for a build up to a great finale. Other hymns followed.

On listening to the fellows sing I could not help but think of the big part the Woodvale and their music has played in the evangelical life of Ulster over these fifty years. For them music is not an industry to entertain the crowds and enrich the singers. Rather, it is a ministry by which they express their praise to the Lord, to edify, to comfort, and to encourage many believers. Singing is also a means by which they seek to reach the lost for Jesus Christ.

Without Alec McCarroll's continued stamina and tenacity for the quartet through these fifty years the Woodvale's ministry might not have been possible. While other members have come and gone Alec has survived for half a century in the service of his Lord and has lost none of his enthusiasm for singing. On occasions one or another member has to miss an engagement because of business or travel. When this happens the other colleagues try to compensate for the missing voice but it is almost unimaginable to have the Woodvale sing without Alec's leadership.

Early in the ministry of the Woodvale Jock McCormick of the Donegall Road Singers greatly encouraged the Woodvale lads of that time to keep at their commitment to singing the gospel. He characteristically but truly said, "There are many mushroom groups that spring up from time to time. Be in this work for the long haul."

Fifty years has been a long haul. Throughout the years the Woodvale have been singing together there has not only been great harmony of voice and music but also good harmony in fellowship and purpose. The personnel may have changed a lot over these years, but the Woodvale have kept their eye on their goal - - singing to please the Saviour and serve in Him in the blessing of saints and sinners. Nowadays they invite several friends to accompany them as guest preachers. Wesley Kane, a gifted preacher from the Branagh Mission, is usually their first choice. Although he was honoured by Her Majesty the Queen for his services rendered to the Belfast shipyard, Wesley has great joy in serving the King of Kings by holding forth the

Word of Life after the Woodvale have presented the gospel in song. On the occasions that Wesley is not able to join them, Trevor Williamson steps in as a competent replacement to assist the Woodvale's musical ministry.

No group of five or more individuals works together without having differing views and sometimes occasional disagreements. Dates for extra meetings can be very inconvenient. Arrangements of various songs may not be what everyone desires. However, the Woodvale boys have enjoyed a blend of fellowship that has enabled them to agree and to disagree in the interests of the over all ministry. Singing for the Woodvale is not looked at as a performance nor is it a professional occupation. It is men's genuine service for their Lord for which they sacrifice their time and to which they give their best commitment.

Often after a meeting people request a copy of the music for a particular arrangement that the Woodvale has sung. They are surprised to find there is no music to hand. The fellows depend on natural pitch and painstaking practice rather than transcribing the music of each piece. This method has worked well for fifty years, and many affirm that seldom is there a variation in tone or pitch.

Perhaps the Woodvale's commitment and dogged determination not to fail on any engagement they make was best illustrated by a trip they made to Scotland where they had planned a weekend of meetings at Hamilton Baptist Church. Just prior to their departure John Gardiner requested to be released from hospital after a very severe burn on his foot. In spite of the pain he was determined to be with the boys. He arrived at the boat with his foot bandaged. John's brother Andrew also arrived at the boat with his leg in plaster and hobbling between two crutches. He was recovering after a cartilage operation on his knee. In spite of their injuries neither of them was prepared to miss the trip. At the Baptist Church it took the lads quite a while to assemble in the pulpit as the handicapped Gardiner brothers awkwardly clambered up and down the pulpit staircase.

The same dedication and commitment to their ministry was shown when George Whitely attended a recording session at Solomen & Peres on the night of his twenty-first wedding anniversary and only arrived home at 10:00 p.m. for the family celebration. His family friends had been celebrating in his absence. Amazingly George and Sadie are still happily married!

Over the last decade the Woodvale had to make more modifications to their approach to singing. For almost forty years the Quintet had been singing without any audio amplification. However, several factors forced them to change. Many churches took full advantage of the modern electronic revolution and installed new audio equipment into their meeting halls and auditorium. Because this new equipment varied so much from place to place it was difficult to be sure of a true and adequate sound system for Quintet singing. In some places the bass voices would drown the tenor and baritone, and on other occasions the opposite would happen.

To sing without the aid of the new sound systems became a virtual impossibility in many places. In the redecoration of churches and mission halls, newly acquired materials were employed to lower ceilings and conserve heat. Floors were carpeted and fancy curtains were often used to adorn windows. All of these elements killed the acoustics which wooden floors and wooden ceilings gave and had a deadening effect on natural sound.

To compensate for these developments it was necessary that the Woodvale provide their own audio equipment. This also meant transporting a lot more accoutrements on their engagements. To store and transport it all it was necessary for the boys to divide the apparatus between themselves and then assemble it in good time for the start of an engagement.

It is impossible to calculate how many miles have been travelled by the Woodvale members over the stretch of fifty years. Back in 1948 the original group travelled to their first engagements on the Belfast double gauge electric trams that now can be found only in the Ulster Transport Museum. Trams gave way to electric trolley buses and double deck buses to single deckers. After a full day's work the singers would only arrive home at almost 6:00 p.m., have a rushed meal, wash and change and then endeavour to catch a bus or even two buses to a venue in the city. When they travelled on the old green buses to rural destinations the four singers filed into the long seat at the rear of the bus and evangelised and entertained the other passengers as they sang all the way to the meeting and all the journey home again.

As times improved in the 1960s Alec McCarroll was the first member to be able to purchase a small car. It was a Ford Anglia which also is a museum piece today. After fifty years of all sorts of transport nearly all members have their family car and transport for people and equipment is no longer a problem.

Amazingly there has never been so much as a minor accident in fifty years. All the fellows agree that this protection must be attributed to the mercy of the Lord and answer to the prayers of many people. Driving a full vehicle to and from meetings through congested city streets on fast motor ways or narrow and unknown country roads with vague direction has called for a lot of praying even as they drive. Surely the Lord has answered those prayers. However, the lads not only pray as they drive but their enthusiasm for their ministry comes through when you discover they still sing all the way to and from the meetings even though there is no public to evangelise as when they travelled on busses.

The ministry of the Woodvale would not have been possible without the patient and generous support of their wives. While the singers have tried to be balanced in booking engagements and planning trips to Scotland and England the ministry does demand time, commitment and help from the fellows' partners. During fifty years the wives have not been wanting in their unstinting cooperation with this ministry. For a short time in the early days of the Woodvale the wives formed their own female quartet and did a few meetings. That did not last too long but the wives have been supportive of each other and often travel to the meetings or functions with their husbands and periodically they have their own social get-togethers.

Throughout the fifty years there have been multiple singers who for varying lengths of time comprised the Woodvale Quintet. Employment, re-location, illness, change of Christian service and even death have all been factors in the change and diversity of singers who have made their contribution to this ministry. Alec McCarroll, however, has been there throughout the whole fifty years and much of the survival and success of the singing group must be put down to Alec's persistence and enthusiasm for their musical ministry. If it is fair to say the Woodvale's music has been Alec's life then his wife Jean must feel she married the Woodvale. It has been their life's work.

How long will this ministry go on? That is an imponderable question. Recently a preacher asked a singer friend how long he will go on singing. The soloist replied, "In heaven your preaching will cease but our song will go on."

> My heart can sing when I pause to remember,
> A heartache here is but a stepping stone;
> Along a trail that's winding ever upwards,
> This troubled world is not my final home.

But until then my heart will go on singing,
Until then with joy I'll carry on,
Until the day my eyes behold the city,
Until the day God calls me home.

The things of earth will dim and lose their value,
If we recall they're borrowed for a while;
And things of earth that cause the heart to tremble,
Remembered there will only bring a smile.

This weary world with all its toil and struggle
May take its toll of misery and strife;
The soul of man is like a waiting falcon,
When it's released it's destined for the skies.